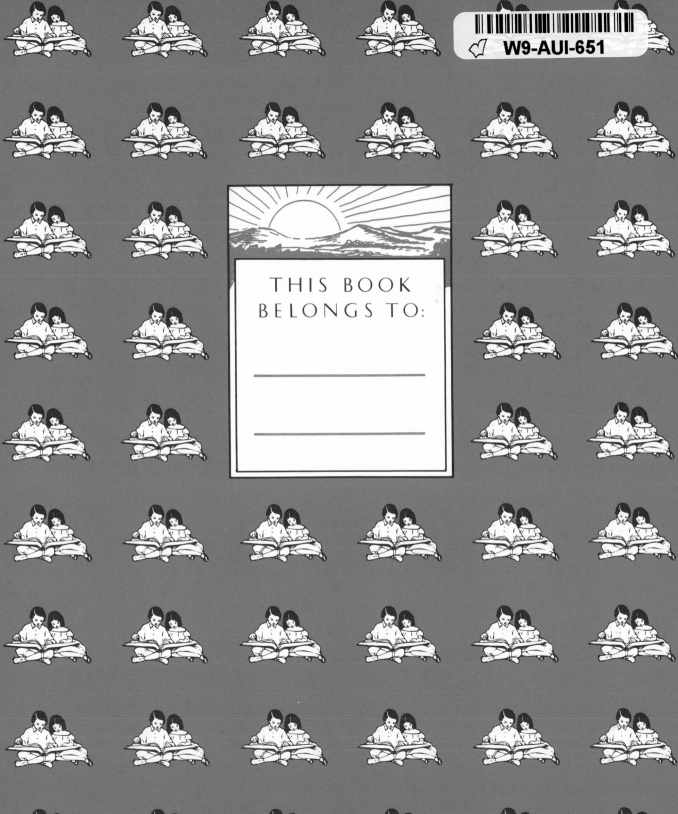

THIS BOOK
BELONGS TO:

_____

_____

ÆSOP'S FABLES

CHILDREN'S CLASSICS

This unique series of Children's Classics™ features accessible and highly readable texts paired with the work of talented and brilliant illustrators of bygone days to create fine editions for today's parents and children to rediscover and treasure. Besides being a handsome addition to any home library, this series features genuine bonded-leather spines stamped in gold, full-color illustrations, and high-quality acid-free paper that will enable these books to be passed from one generation to the next.

ÆSOP'S FABLES

Illustrated by Nora Fry

Edited by Lois Hill

CHILDREN'S CLASSICS

NEW YORK • AVENEL, NEW JERSEY

This 1989 edition is published by Children's Classics, a
division of dilithium Press, Ltd., distributed by Outlet Book
Company, Inc., a Random House Company, 40 Engelhard
Avenue, Avenel, New Jersey 07001.

DILITHIUM is a registered trademark and
CHILDREN'S CLASSICS is a trademark of dilithium Press, Ltd.

Printed and bound in the United States of America.

ISBN 0-517-67901-9
10 9 8 7 6

Library of Congress Cataloging-in-Publication Data

Aesop's fables.
  Aesop's fables / illustrated by Nora Fry ; edited by Lois Hill.
      p.   cm. — (Children's classics)
    Reprint.
    Includes index.
    Summary: Presents an illustrated collection of moral
  tales from Aesop.
    ISBN 0-517-67901-9 (alk. paper)
    1. Fables. [1. Fables.] I. Fry, Nora, ill. II. Hill, Lois.
  III. Title. IV. Series.
  PZ8.2.A254   1989b
  398.2′452—dc19   88-39113
                                                         CIP
                                                          AC

CONTENTS

Introduction . . . .*xvii*

Angler and the Little Fish, The 117

Ant and the Dove, The 58

Ant and the Grasshopper, The 23

Ants, The 145

Apes and the Travellers, The 45

Arab and the Camel, The 43

Archer and the Lion, The 166

Ass and his Burdens, The 191

Ass and his Master, The 24

Ass and his Purchaser, The 163

Ass and the Frogs, The 179

Ass and the Grasshopper, The 114

Ass and the Lap-Dog, The 65

Ass in the Lion's Skin, The 123

v

Contents

Ass's Brains, The 156

Ass, the Cock, and the Lion, The 131

Ass, The Fox, and the Lion, The 11

Bat and the Weasels, The 135

Bat, the Bramble, and the Seagull, The . . .175

Bear and the Fox, The 134

Bee and Jupiter, The 169

Bee Keeper, The 144

Bees, the Drones, and the Wasp, The 95

Birdcatcher, the Partridge, and the Cock, The 180

Blacksmith and his Dog, The 189

Blind Man and the Cub, The 189

Bull and the Goat, The 107

Bundle of Sticks, The 31

Cat and the Birds, The 152

Cat and the Cock, The 150

Cat and the Fox, The 93

Cat and the Mice, The 38

Cat-Maiden, The 202

Charger and the Ass, The 84

Cock and the Jewels, The 21

Country Maid and her Milk-Pail, The 61

Countryman and the Snake, The 78

Crab and his Mother, The 84

Contents

Crab and the Fox, The 167

Creaking Wheels, The 132

Crow and the Pitcher, The 34

Crow and the Raven, The 139

Dog and the Hare, The 167

Dog and the Oyster, The 173

Dog and the Shadow, The 36

Dog and the Wolf, The 158

Dog in the Manger, The 14

Dog Invited to Supper, The 52

Dog, the Cock, and the Fox, The 67

Dogs and the Hides, The 30

Eagle and the Arrow, The 65

Eagle and the Beetle, The 97

Eagle and the Fox, The 146

Eagle and the Jackdaw, The 99

Eagle and the Lion, The 151

Farmer and the Dogs, The 121

Farmer and the Fox, The 154

Farmer and the Snake, The 183

Farmer and the Stork, The 192

Fatal Marriage, The 56

Fawn and her Mother, The 60

Fighting Cocks and the Eagle, The 40

Contents

Fisherman and the Little Fish, The 171

Fisherman, The 57

Flea and the Man, The 169

Flies and the Honey-Pot, The 57

Fox and the Crow, The 110

Fox and the Goat, The 12

Fox and the Grapes, The 127

Fox and the Lion, The 15

Fox and the Mask, The 133

Fox and the Monkey, The 23

Fox and the Mosquitoes, The 184

Fox and the Stork, The 91

Fox and the Woodman, The 130

Fox Who Lost his Tail, The 51

Frog and the Ox, The 26

Frogs' Complaint against the Sun, The . . .137

Gnat and the Bull, The 149

Gnat and the Lion, The 176

Goat and the Goatherd, The 198

Goose with the Golden Eggs, The 112

Hare and the Tortoise, The 21

Hare with Many Friends, The 139

Hares and the Frogs, The 41

Hawk and the Nightingale, The 168

Contents

Hawk, the Kite, and the Pigeons, The 193

Hedge and the Vineyard, The 128

Hen and the Cat, The 47

Hercules and the Carter 126

Horse and the Lion, The 77

Horse and the Miller, The 141

Horse and the Stag, The 77

Hound and the Hare, The 43

House-Dog and the Wolf, The 101

Hunter and the Woodman, The 144

Huntsman and the Fisherman, The 161

Husbandman and the Stork, The 33

Jupiter, Neptune, Minerva, and Momus 28

Kid and the Wolf, The 20

King Log and King Stork 59

Kite, the Frog, and the Mouse, The 82

Kites and the Swans, The 149

Lamb and the Wolf, The 85

Lamb Chased by a Wolf, The 154

Lamp, The 203

Lark and her Young Ones, The 108

Leopard and the Fox, The 9

Leopard and the Three Bulls, The 64

Lion and his Three Counsellors, The 113

Contents

Lion and the Boar, The 73

Lion and the Fox, The 194

Lion and the Frog, The 160

Lion and the Mouse, The 54

Lion and the Statue, The 200

Lion and the Three Bulls, The 171

Lion in Love, The 18

Lion, the Bear, and the Fox, The 71

Lion, the Fox, and the Beasts, The 136

Lion, the Mouse, and the Fox, The 186

Lioness, The 111

Man and his Two Wives, The 106

Man and the Serpent, The 165

Master and his Dogs, The 182

Mice and the Weasels, The 197

Mice in Council, The 16

Miller, his Son, and their Ass, The 88

Mischievous Dog, The 32

Mole and her Mother, The 92

Monkey and the Camel, The 76

Monkey as King, The 201

Moon and her Mother, The 25

Mountains in Labour, The 158

Mouse and the Bull, The 181

Contents

Mouse and the Weasel, The 119

Mouse, the Frog, and the Hawk, The 199

Mule, The 101

Nightingale and the Swallow, The 138

Nurse and the Wolf, The 105

Oak and the Reeds, The 116

Oak and the Woodcutters, The 162

Old Hound, The 29

Old Woman and her Maids, The 63

One-Eyed Doe, The 164

Owl and the Birds, The 142

Oxen and the Butchers, The 81

Peacock and Juno, The 159

Peacock and the Crane, The 151

Peasant and the Apple Tree, The 147

Pig and the Sheep, The 87

Pomegranate, the Apple Tree, and the
 Bramble, The 170

Quack Frog, The 120

Rivers and the Sea, The 193

Rose and the Amaranth, The 196

Serpent and the Eagle, The 155

She-Goats and their Beards, The 187

Shepherd and the Sheep, The 174

Contents

Shepherd-Boy and the Wolf, The 35

Sick Stag, The 37

Sick Wolf and the Lamb, The 118

Spendthrift and the Swallow, The 142

Stag and the Lion, The 183

Stag and the Vine, The 177

Stag at the Pool, The 123

Stag in the Ox-Stall, The 195

Swallow and the Crow, The 156

Swallow and the Other Birds, The 190

Swallow, the Serpent, and the Court of

   Justice, The 179

Swan and the Goose, The 145

Thief and his Mother, The 79

Thief and the Yard Dog, The 104

Thirsty Pigeon, The 153

Tortoise and the Eagle, The 75

Town Mouse and the Country Mouse, The . . 5

Traveller and his Dog, The 177

Travellers and the Bear, The 74

Travellers and the Plane-Tree, The 162

Trees and the Axe, The 72

Trees under the Protection of the Gods, The . . 197

Two Frogs, The 184

Contents

Two Pots, The 17

Two Travellers and the Axe, The 152

Vain Jackdaw, The 50

Viper and the File, The 173

Wanton Calf, The 69

Widow and the Hen, The 125

Widow and the Sheep, The 188

Wild Boar and the Fox, The 129

Wind and the Sun, The 48

Wolf and the Crane, The 13

Wolf and the Goat, The 115

Wolf and the Horse, The 163

Wolf and the Lamb, The 8

Wolf and the Lion, The 126

Wolf and the Shepherd, The 96

Wolf in Sheep's Clothing, The 122

Wolf, the Fox, and the Ape, The 148

Wolves and the Dogs, The 187

ILLUSTRATIONS
IN COLOR

FACING PAGE

The Mice in Council 12

The Ass and His Master 13

The Vain Jackdaw 44

King Log and King Stork 45

Hercules and the Carter 76

The Tortoise and the Eagle 77

The Fox and the Crow 108

The Fox and the Grapes 109

INTRODUCTION

In asking "Who was Aesop?" we are, in a sense, demanding to be told the impossible. There are as many stories about Aesop as there are fables by him, and as many fables as there are translations and interpretations of them. That is to say, the possibilities of Aesop are endless, timeless, and extraordinary. What secrets are hidden within his name?

As the historians would have it, Aesop was a rare man indeed. Born a slave in Phrygia, a country of Asia Minor, during the golden age of ancient Greece, he learned to read and write, and won his freedom by means of his wit and skill with words. Soon recognized as an important Phrygian philosopher, he traveled widely throughout Greece and Egypt, finally settling at the court of Croesus, King of Lydia, who became his greatest patron.

Just as there are many ironies in Aesop's stories, so does his life affirm the often swift changes of fortune. On behalf of King Croesus, Aesop undertook a mission to the Oracle at Delphi. There, he deeply offended the people of Delphi by comparing them to sticks floating on the sea, which appear great at a distance, and turn out to be nothing when brought near. To punish him for his sarcasm, the Delphians accused Aesop of stealing one of the sacred vessels from Apollo's temple, and for this affront he was thrown off the edge of a cliff, and died.

About 300 B.C., some two hundred fifty years after Aesop's untimely demise, the Athenian tyrant Demetrius Phalereus (also the founder of the Alexandrian Library) compiled what is believed to have been the first written collection of *Aesop's Fables*. It is from this work, now lost, that the "modern" Aesop is derived.

This is one way to tell Aesop's story. There are many other ways. In working with this collection of *Aesop's Fables*, I discovered that there is, in fact, no limit to the theme and variations on the universal truths about which Aesop wrote. I also discovered the meaning concealed in Aesop's name. Just as I can look at the name "Odysseus," the hero of Homer's epic poem *The Odyssey*, and tell you that his name means "the wanderer"—a true and fitting description for this hero and the work itself, so can I also show you that Aesop's name, in the original language of his stories, means "eternal voice" or "timeless word." The parable of Aesop's name is, in fact, at the core of his timeless and eternal fables—it is the truth hidden in delightful disguise.

Here is the philosopher concealed in the "sheep's clothing" of a storyteller. Aesop hid the true nature of mankind, as he saw us, from the critical eyes of those who would censor him, disguising these truths in stories peopled by animals, gods, men, and even inanimate objects. His fables are among the great satirical and anthropomorphic animal stories, stories such as men and women of genius create from time to time to show the human condition. When, and often out of necessity, this writing takes the form of a story, or a narrative composed of stories (such as Jonathan Swift's *Gulliver's Travels*), then we truly possess an extraordinary work, one that may be read by all ages, and that transcends all ages.

Aesop's Fables encompasses the whole of the animal kingdom, from the tiniest of mice to the largest and fiercest of lions. Certain animals, or as we should say, certain characters, appear more frequently than others, and among the most common is the fox, sly Reynard (the French name for "fox") who is given to tricking the other animals, often for his own pleasure, and will not freely admit discomfort or defeat. There is also the evil wolf, both greedy and treacherous, a menace to both animals and men; the ass, humble bearer of burdens for man and otherwise notable among the animals for his lack of intelligence; the mouse, a small but intensely active creature whose well-meaning but often poorly planned activities bring extra trouble upon it; and the lion, king of the beasts, whose strength and cunning combine to give him the power and authority of rule.

Here is a world where animals, birds, and gods all become human in every way but their shapes. Each creature must bear the limitations of his natural shape and abode, but (as we humans do) also assume the responsibility for his actions—both for himself and for others. *Aesop's Fables* are stories written to instruct and to entertain. Simply constructed, they lead quickly and concisely to a natural end. Action is balanced by reaction; ignorance is countered by thought. These are stories harmonious in flow but not always in outcome. For the laws of nature are fierce, and the truism "eat or be eaten" predominates.

Certain of *Aesop's Fables* are so well known that they have become part of our contemporary oral tradition. "The Goose with the Golden Eggs" is everyone's pipe dream of instant wealth, and teaches the lesson *'Let well alone.'* In "The Town Mouse and the Country Mouse," the splendors of civilization are revealed to the innocent:

> "Here were couches of crimson velvet, carvings in ivory, everything, in short, that told of wealth and ease. On the table were the remains of a splendid meal, and it was now the turn of the town mouse to play the host: he ran to and fro to supply his friend's wants, pressed dish upon dish and dainty upon dainty, and, as though he were waiting upon a king, tasted every course before placing it before his rustic cousin."

But when their dinner is unexpectedly interrupted, these exotic treats are hastily discarded in favor of the security of a simpler country life.

"The Crow and the Pitcher" illustrates the effectiveness of need and ingenuity in solving the "unsolvable" problem, and bears the epigram: *'Necessity is the mother of invention.'* And "The Wolf in Sheep's Clothing" has found its way into classic fairy tales such as *Little Red Riding Hood.*

Other fables are less common, but just as poignant. In "The Horse and the Miller," an old horse receives good advice, and little consolation, from the miller for whom he is working after retiring from the battlefield:

> "'Cease,' said the miller to him, 'from dwelling upon the past, for it is the common fate of men to bear the ups and downs of fortune.'"

Typical of stories blending both animals and gods is "The Bee and Jupiter," where a honeybee is granted her wish to possess a sting, in return for which she must give her life. Though changed, the essential balance of nature is not altered by the wisdom of the gods. Aesop's gods are the gods of ancient Greece and Rome. Although they bear the names of the Roman gods, their behavior is every bit as human as that of the great Greek gods of Homer; foil and counterfoil for the men, they are above yet within everything.

The penultimate story in this collection is entitled "The Cat-Maiden." Atypical in that it suggests that matter may be transformed, it illustrates the key theme running throughout the fables—that nature may not be changed. In conclusion, our final story speaks of that greatest of human frailties, vanity:

> "A lamp, soaked with too much oil, and flaring very much, boasted that he gave more light than even the sun. A sudden puff of wind arising, he was immediately extinguished. His owner lit him again, and said, 'Boast no more, but henceforth be content to give your light in silence. Know that not even the stars need to be relit.'"

In *Aesop's Fables* we observe the adventures of creatures great and small, and find pleasure over and over again in these stories which so marvelously show us our own nature set within the unity of the whole.

LOIS HILL

New York
1988

The Town Mouse and the Country Mouse

ONCE upon a time a country mouse who had a friend in town invited him, for the sake of old times, to pay him a visit in the country.

The invitation being accepted in due course, the country mouse, though plain and rough in his habits of living, opened his heart in honour of an old friend. There was not a carefully stored-up morsel that he did not bring forth out of his larder—peas and barley, cheese-parings and nuts—hoping by quantity to make up what he feared was wanting in quality.

The town mouse, who was used to more dainty fare, at first picked a bit here and a bit

there, while the host sat nibbling a blade of
barley straw.

At length he exclaimed, "How is it, my good
friend, that you can endure the
dullness of this life? You are
living like a toad in a hole. You
can't really prefer these lonely rocks
and woods to streets filled with
shops and carriages and men!
Believe me, you are wasting your
time here. We must make the
most of life while it lasts. A
mouse, you know, does not live
for ever. So come with me, and
I'll show you life and the town."

These fine words were too much for the simple
country mouse, and he agreed to go with his
friend to town.

It was late in the evening when the two crept
into the city, and midnight ere they reached the
great house where the town mouse lived. Here
were couches of crimson velvet, carvings in ivory,
everything, in short, that told of wealth and ease.
On the table were the remains of a splendid meal,
and it was now the turn of the town mouse to play

6

the host : he ran to and fro to supply his friend's wants, pressed dish upon dish and dainty upon dainty, and, as though he were waiting on a king, tasted every course before placing it before his rustic cousin.

The country mouse, for his part, tried to appear quite at home, and blessed the good fortune that had brought such a change in his way of life ; when, in the midst of his enjoyment, as he was wondering how he could have been content with the poor fare he was used to at home, on a sudden the door opened and a party of ladies and gentlemen, returning from the theatre, entered the room.

The two friends jumped from the table in the greatest fright, and hid themselves in the first corner they could reach. When the room was quiet again they ventured to creep out, but the barking of dogs drove them back in still greater terror than before.

At length, when all the household was asleep, the country mouse stole out from his hiding-place, and, bidding his host good-bye, whispered in his ear, " My good friend, this fine mode of living may do for those who like it ; but give me barley bread in peace and security before the daintiest feast where Fear and Care lie in wait."

A humble life with peace and quiet is better than a splendid one with danger and risk.

The Wolf and the Lamb

As a wolf was drinking at the head of a running brook he saw a stray lamb paddling at some distance down the stream. Having made up his mind to eat her for his supper, he wondered what excuse he could make for a quarrel.

"Villain!" said he, running up to her, "how dare you spoil the water that I am drinking?"

"Indeed," said the lamb humbly, "I do not see how I can spoil the water, since it runs from you to me, not from me to you."

"That is all very well," replied the wolf; "it

is but a year since you called me many nasty names!"

"Oh, sir," said the lamb, trembling, "a year ago I was not born!"

"Well," replied the wolf, "if it was not you, it was your father, and that is all the same; but it is no use trying to talk me out of my supper"; and without another word he fell upon the poor helpless lamb and tore her to pieces.

The tyrant will always find an excuse when
he would injure the innocent.

The Leopard and the Fox

ONE day a leopard, feeling very proud of his beautiful spots, went so far as to ask himself why even the lion should be thought greater than he, who had so rare a skin. Indeed, so proud did he become that he made up his mind to have nothing to do with other beasts of the forest.

This, of course, was soon noticed, and the fox, feeling very hurt and annoyed, went boldly up to the leopard and told him that he was foolish in having such a good opinion of himself.

"You may think yourself very fine," said Reynard, "but, depend upon it, people value a bright brain far more than a handsome body."

Beauty is only skin-deep.

The Ass, the Fox, and the Lion

THE ass and the fox entered into partnership together to protect each other, and swore eternal friendship. Soon after they went a-hunting, but before they had gone far a lion crossed their path. The fox saw the lion first, and, pointing him out to the ass, said, "We must make terms with this lion and get him to be friendly with us." So saying, he went boldly up to the lion and offered to help him secure the ass, provided that his own life should be spared. The lion was quite willing to promise this, whereupon the fox induced the ass to follow him to a deep pit, into which he managed to push him. As soon as the lion saw that the ass was secured he sprang upon the fox and made a meal of him, leaving the ass to be eaten at his leisure.

Those who betray their friends must not expect others to keep faith with them.

The Fox and the Goat

ONE day a fox fell into a well, and wondered for a long time how he could get out again. At last a goat came along, and, feeling very thirsty, he asked Reynard if the water was good and if there was plenty of it.

The fox now saw his chance, and, pretending that he was swimming for pleasure, replied, "Yes, come down, my friend; the water is so nice that I cannot drink enough of it, and there is plenty for both of us."

So the goat jumped in without a thought, and the artful fox, making use of his friend's horns, quickly sprang out.

Then when he was safely on top of the well he coolly remarked to the poor goat, "Had

The Mice in Council

Page 16

The Ass and His Master

Page 24

you half as much brains as you have beard, you would have looked before you leaped."

Think before you act.

The Wolf and the Crane

A WOLF had got a bone stuck in his throat, and being in great pain ran howling up and down, begging every animal he met to relieve him, at the same time hinting at a very handsome reward to the one who succeeded in getting it out.

A crane, feeling sorry for him, and being tempted by his promises, put her long beak down the wolf's throat and drew out the bone. She then modestly asked for the promised reward.

But the wolf, grinning and

showing his teeth and pretending to feel hurt, replied, "You ungrateful creature! Have I not given you your life? I had your head in my mouth and could have bitten it off whenever I pleased. How many can say they have had their head in a wolf's jaws and brought it safely out again? And yet you are not content!"

Those who expect thanks from rascals
are often disappointed.

The Dog in the Manger

A DOG once made his bed in a manger, and lay snarling and growling to keep the horses away from their food.

"What a miserable cur he is!" said one of the animals. "He cannot eat the corn himself nor will he let us eat it who are hungry."

Live and let live.

The Fox and the Lion

WHEN a fox who had never seen a lion met one
for the first time he was so terrified that he
almost died of fright. When he met him the
second time, however, he was still afraid, but
managed to hide his fear. But when he saw
him for the third time he felt so brave that he
went up and began to talk to him as though
they were old friends.

Familiarity breeds contempt.

The Mice in Council

ONCE upon a time a number of mice called a meeting to decide upon the best means of ridding themselves of a cat that had killed so many of their friends and relations. Various plans were discussed and rejected, until at last a young mouse came forward and proposed that a bell should be hung round the tyrant's neck, that they might, in future, have warning of her movements and so be able to escape.

The suggestion was received joyfully by nearly all, but an old mouse, who had sat silent for some time, got up and said: "While I consider the plan to be a very clever one, and feel sure that it would prove to be quite successful if carried out, I should like to know who is going to bell the cat."

It is easier to make a suggestion than to carry it out.

The Two Pots

Two pots, one of earthenware and the other of brass, were carried down a river together on the tide. The brass pot promised his companion that if she would keep by his side he would protect her.

"Thank you for the offer," said the other, "but that is just what I do not want to do. If you will only keep at a distance I may float down in safety, but should we come together I am sure to be the sufferer."

Too powerful neighbours should be avoided,
for if a quarrel occurs the weaker
goes to the wall.

The Lion in Love

MANY years ago, even before your great-great-grandparents were born, a lion fell in love with a woodcutter's daughter, and begged that he might be given her hand in marriage.

The woodcutter was not at all pleased with the offer, and declined the honour of so dangerous a son-in-law. Whereupon the lion became very angry and threatened to use force if his suit was denied.

The poor man, seeing that the dangerous creature was in earnest, hit upon a plan whereby he could gain his ends without risking his life.

"I feel greatly flattered by your proposal," said he, "but, noble sir, what great teeth you have! and what long claws! Where is the damsel that would not be alarmed by such frightful weapons! You must have your teeth drawn and your claws cut before you can hope to be accepted as a suitable bridegroom for my daughter."

So madly was the lion in love that he fell into

18

the trap and sat quietly while the operation was being performed. He then claimed the daughter for his bride.

But the woodcutter was no longer afraid of his unwelcome visitor; he seized a stout stick and drove him from the door.

Misfortune will surely befall him who loves unwisely.

The Kid and the Wolf

A KID standing on the tiled roof of a tall house saw a wolf pass below, and began to speak very

rudely to him.   The wolf stopped only to reply, "Coward! it is not you who insult me, but the place on which you are standing."

It is easy to be brave when far away
from danger.

The Cock and the Jewels

As a cock was scratching up the straw in a farm-yard, looking for food for his hens, he came across a string of pearls that somehow had found its way there.

"Ho!" said he, "you are a very fine thing, no doubt, to those who like you; but give me a barley-corn before all the pearls in the world."

Silly people despise what is precious because they cannot understand it.

The Hare and the Tortoise

A HARE met a tortoise one day and made fun of him for the slow and clumsy way in which he walked.

The tortoise laughed and said, "I will run a race with you any time that you choose."

"Very well," replied the hare, "we will start at once."

The tortoise immediately set off in his slow and steady way without waiting a moment or looking back.   The hare, on the other hand, treated the matter as a joke and decided to take a little nap before starting, for she thought that it would be an easy matter to overtake her rival.

The tortoise plodded on, and meanwhile the hare overslept herself, with the result that she arrived at the winning-post only to see that the tortoise had got in before her.

Slow and steady wins the race.

The Ant and the Grasshopper

ON a cold frosty day an ant which had laid up some corn in the summer-time was bringing it out to dry.

A grasshopper, half dead with hunger, begged the ant to give him a morsel to preserve his life.

"What were you doing," asked the ant, "all through last summer?"

"Oh," said the grasshopper, "I was not idle. I sang all day long."

The ant laughed and, collecting her grain, said, "Since you could sing all the summer, you may dance all the winter."

We should never lose a good opportunity.

The Fox and the Monkey

A MONKEY once danced in an assembly of the beasts, and so greatly pleased all by his performance that they elected him their king.

A fox who envied him the honour, having discovered a piece of meat lying in a trap, led the monkey to the tit-bit and said:

"Look! I have found this store, but have not used it. It is not for the subject to lay claim to treasure trove; the king himself should take it."

The monkey approached carelessly and was caught in the trap, whereupon he accused the fox of purposely leading him into the snare.

The fox replied, "O monkey, and can it be that you, with so simple a mind, could rule as king over the beasts?"

The simple are easily deceived.

The Ass and his Master

An ass that was being driven along the road bolted from his master, and, leaving the beaten track, made as fast as he could for the edge of a precipice. He was upon the point of falling over when his master ran up and, seizing him by the tail, endeavoured to pull him into safety. But the ass, resenting his master's interference, pulled the opposite way, and the man was forced to let go his hold.

"Well, Jack," said he, "if you will be master,
I cannot stop you."

A wilful beast must go his own way.

The Moon and her Mother

THE moon once asked her mother to make her a
cloak that would fit her well. "How," replied
she, "can I make a cloak to fit you when you are
first a new moon, then a full moon, and then
neither one nor the other?"

Changeable people are not easily satisfied.

The Frog and the Ox

An ox, grazing in a swampy meadow, happened to put his foot on a family of young frogs and crushed most of them to death.

Now, one that escaped ran off to his mother with the dreadful news.

"Oh, Mother!" he said, "while we were playing, such a big four-footed beast trod on us."

"Big?" asked the old frog; "how big? Was it as big"—and she puffed herself out very much—"as big as this?"

"Oh!" said the little one, "a great deal bigger than that."

"Well, was it so big?" and she swelled herself out still more.

"Yes, Mother, it was; and if you were to swell till you burst yourself you would never be half its size."

Annoyed with her little one for doubting her powers, the old frog tried yet again, and this time burst herself in the vain attempt.

Men may be ruined by attempting to appear that which Nature has not intended them to be.

Jupiter, Neptune, Minerva, and Momus

JUPITER, Neptune, and Minerva, so we are told, were unable to agree as to which of them could make the most perfect thing, and so they asked Momus, who, you may remember, was the god of laughter, to decide for them.

Jupiter made a man, Minerva made a house, and Neptune made a bull.

When the time came for Momus to judge he first found fault with the bull because its horns were not below its eyes.

"It would not be able," he said, "to see when it butted with them!"

He then complained that the man had no window in his chest.

28

"Nobody," said he, "would be able to read his thoughts!"

Lastly, he found fault with the house because it had no wheels.

"People who live in this house," he said, "could not move from place to place away from unpleasant neighbours."

Then Jupiter lost patience and drove Momus out of Olympus, declaring angrily that nobody could ever please a fault-finder, and that it would be well for Momus to make something really good himself before he again found fault with the work of others.

Be reasonable in your criticism.

The Old Hound

A HOUND who had been most skilled and faithful to his master in the hunting-field at last became too old to continue to play his part as in his younger days.

One day, when hunting a wild boar, he seized the creature by the ear, but not having sufficient strength to retain his hold he allowed the boar to escape.

At that moment his master rode up and, seeing what had happened, severely scolded the dog,

and would have beaten him had he not sadly cried :

"Spare your old servant! Although my heart is willing my limbs are feeble. Remember what I was rather than what I am now."

Faithful service should be long remembered.

The Dogs and the Hides

SOME hungry dogs, unable to reach a number of hides which a skinner had left at the bottom of a stream, agreed among themselves to drink up the river that thereby they might get at their prize. They set to work accordingly, but burst themselves with drinking without coming an inch nearer the hides.

Those who employ unreasonable means to obtain their objects are apt to ruin themselves in the attempt.

The Bundle of Sticks

An old man had many sons who were continually quarrelling together. He had exerted his authority and employed many means in order to reconcile them, but all to no purpose. At last he thought of a plan whereby he would show them the folly of their ways.

Ordering his sons to be called before him, and a bundle of sticks to be brought, he commanded them, one by one, to try if, with all their strength, they could any of them break it. They all tried without success, for the sticks, being closely bound together, could not be broken by the strength of man.

The father next ordered the bundle to be untied, and gave a single stick to each of his sons, at the same time bidding him try to break it, which, of course, each did with the greatest of ease.

"Oh, my sons," said the father, "behold the power of unity. If you would live together in friendship your enemies would be unable to harm you, but when once the ties of brotherly affection are broken you are likely to suffer from every unfriendly hand that is turned against you."

Unity is strength.

The Mischievous Dog

THERE was a dog so wild and mischievous that his master was obliged to fasten a bell about his neck, to warn his neighbours of his bad character.

The dog, priding himself upon his ornament, paraded in the market-place, shaking his bell to attract attention. But a little dog, who had listened to the remarks round him, cried, " The less noise you make the better; your bell is only to give you a bad character with your neighbours, and is nothing to pride yourself on."

Men often mistake notoriety for fame.

The Husbandman and the Stork

FINDING that cranes were destroying his newly sown corn, a farmer one evening set a net in his field to catch the destructive birds. When he went to examine the net next morning he found a number of cranes in its meshes, also a stork.

" Release me, I beseech you," cried the stork, "for I have eaten none of your corn, nor have

I done you any harm. I am a poor innocent stork, as you may see—a most dutiful bird. I honour my father and mother. I——"

But the farmer cut him short. "All this may be true enough, I dare say, but I have caught you with those who were destroying my crops, and you must suffer with the company in which you are found.

People are judged by the company they keep.

The Crow and the Pitcher

A CROW was almost dying of thirst when he spied a pitcher at no great distance. When he came

up to it, however, he found that it was nearly empty; the little water in it was so low that, try as he might, he was unable to reach it. Thereupon he tried to break the pitcher, then to overturn it, but his strength was not sufficient to do one or the other.

At last, seeing a number of small pebbles close by, he took these and dropped them, one by one, into the pitcher until the water rose to the brim and he was able to quench his thirst.

Necessity is the mother of invention.

The Shepherd-boy and the Wolf

A SHEPHERD-BOY, who tended his flock not far from a village, often amused himself by crying, "Wolf! wolf!" so that he might laugh at those who came to his assistance. The trick had succeeded several times, until one day the boy had need to cry "Wolf! wolf!" in earnest. Then he learned, when it was too late, that liars are not believed even when they tell the truth, for the villagers, supposing him to be at his tricks again, paid no attention to his cries, and the wolf carried off one of the sheep.

He who tells lies is not believed even when he speaks the truth.

The Dog and the Shadow

A DOG had stolen a piece of meat out of a butcher's shop, and was crossing a river on his way home when he saw his own reflection in the stream below. Thinking that it was another dog, with a larger piece of meat in his mouth, he made up his mind to get that also; but in snapping at the shadow he dropped the meat he was carrying, and so lost all.

He who grasps at the shadow may lose the substance.

The Sick Stag

A STAG, feeling unwell, lay down on the rich and shady grass close by a wood, so that he might obtain his food without effort.

Now many of the other forest animals were fond of him because of his quiet and gentle nature, and thinking that he would feel very lonely, they came one by one to see him.

Each visitor ate a little of the grass, with the

result that before very long none was left for the poor stag. True, he was somewhat cheered by his friends, but as he was now unable to get nourishment he lost both his food and his life.

Thoughtless friends are often a nuisance.

The Cat and the Mice

A CAT grown feeble with age, and no longer able to hunt mice as she had done in her younger days, thought of a way to entice them within reach of her paws.

She suspended herself by the hind legs from

a peg, thinking that the mice would mistake her for a bag, or for a dead cat at the least, and would then venture to come near her.

An old mouse, who was wise enough to keep his distance, whispered to a friend, "Many a bag have I seen in my time, but never one with a cat's head."

"Hang there, good madam," said the other, "as long as you please, but I would not trust myself within reach of you though you were stuffed with straw."

Old birds are not to be caught with chaff.

The Fighting Cocks and the Eagle

Two young cocks, as young cocks usually will, fought long and fiercely for the possession of a coveted dunghill. At last one was

badly beaten and crept away to the corner of the hen-house, broken in pride and spirit, and no longer inclined to challenge his rival. The other, however, having proved himself to be cock of the roost, flew to the top of a fence, and, flapping his wings and crowing, announced his victory to the world. At that moment an eagle, chancing to pass overhead, saw the proud bird. Swooping down he seized him in his talons and carried him away, whereupon the other cock came out from his corner and took possession of the dunghill for which the two had fought.

Pride goes before a fall.

The Hares and the Frogs

A COLONY of hares, made desperate by their many enemies, decided that they would get rid of their troubles by ending their lives. They therefore made their way to a lake near by with the intention of drowning themselves, as the most miserable creatures in the world.

41

Now it happened that a number of frogs were seated on the bank, and these were so frightened at the approach of the hares that they leaped one and all into the water in the greatest confusion.

"Our case is not so hopeless after all," said one of the hares, "for here are other poor creatures more faint-hearted than ourselves."

*Be sure that there are others worse off
than yourself.*

The Hound and the Hare

A HOUND after chasing a hare for a long time came up to her and commenced first to bite and then to lick her. The poor hare, not knowing what to make of his actions, said: "If you are a friend, why do you bite me? If a foe, why caress me?"

Better a certain enemy than a doubtful friend.

The Arab and the Camel

AN Arab, having loaded his camel, asked him whether he preferred to go uphill or downhill.

"Why do you ask, master?" said the camel dryly. "Is the level way across the plain shut up?"

Of what use is it to pretend there is a choice when there is none?

The Fisherman

A FISHERMAN went to a river to fish, and, when he had laid his nets across the stream, he tied a stone to a long cord and beat the water on both sides of the net in order to drive the fish into the meshes. While he was thus employed a cottager who lived close by came up to him and complained that he was disturbing the stream and making the water so muddy that it was unfit to drink.

"I am sorry that this does not please you," said the fisherman, "but it is by thus troubling the waters that I gain my living."

Live and let live.

The Vain Jackdaw

Page 50

King Log and King Stork

Page 59

The Apes and the Travellers

Two men, one of whom always spoke the truth while the other told nothing but lies, were travelling together, and by chance came to the land of apes.

One of the apes, who had raised himself to be king, commanded them to be laid hold of and brought before him, that he might know what was said of him among men.

He ordered, at the same time, that all the apes should be ranged in a long row on his right hand and on his left, and that a throne should be placed for him in the middle, as was the custom among men.

After these preparations the ape signified his will that the two men should be brought before him, and greeted them thus:

"What sort of a king do I seem to you to be, O Strangers?"

The untruthful traveller replied, "You seem to me a most mighty king."

"And what do you think of those you see around me?"

"These," the traveller answered, "are worthy

companions of yourself, fit at least to be ambassadors and leaders of armies."

The ape and all his court were gratified with the flattery, and the king commanded a handsome present to be given to the man.

The truthful traveller now thought within himself, "If so great a reward be given for a lie, with what gift may I not be rewarded if, according to my custom, I tell the truth?" When, therefore, the ape turned to him and asked,

"And, pray, how do I and these my friends around me seem to you?"

"Thou art," he answered boldly, "a most excellent ape, and all these thy companions after thy example are excellent apes too."

The king of the apes at hearing these truths flew into a great rage and gave the unfortunate man over to the teeth and claws of his companions.

It is dangerous to speak the truth to tyrants.

The Hen and the Cat

A CAT, hearing that a hen lay sick in her nest, paid her a visit, and creeping up to her said: "How are you, my dear friend? Can I do anything for you? If there is anything you are in want of, let me know and I will bring it to you; but whatever you do, keep up your spirits and don't be alarmed."

"Thank you," said the hen; "but if you will be good enough to leave me I have no doubt that I shall soon be well again."

Unbidden guests quickly outstay their welcome.

The Wind and the Sun

A DISPUTE once arose between the north wind and the sun as to which of them was the more powerful.

Unable to agree, they decided to see which of them could get a cloak from off the back of a traveller on the road beneath them.

48

The north wind started the contest, and sent a strong cold blast to try to blow the garment away. Instead of this making the man cast his cloak, however, it caused him to wind it about his body more closely than ever.

The sun laughed at his opponent's failure, and, exerting his power to the utmost, he drove the thick, watery clouds from the sky and darted his beams upon the head of the poor weather-beaten traveller.

Growing faint with the heat, and at last unable to endure it any longer, the man first threw off his cloak and then made for the shade of some trees which grew near the wayside.

Persuasion is better than force.

The Vain Jackdaw

A JACKDAW, as vain and conceited as a jackdaw could be, picked up some feathers which the peacocks had shed, stuck them among his own, and, despising his old companions, mingled boldly with a flock of the more beautiful birds.

The peacocks instantly turned upon the foolish intruder, stripped him of his borrowed plumes, and drove him away with fierce pecks from their sharp beaks.

The unlucky jackdaw, sorely punished and very downcast, returned to his natural companions, and would have lived with them again as if nothing had happened.

But, remembering how rudely he had behaved, the other jackdaws would no longer have him in their society. One of their number said:

"Had you been contented with what Nature made you, you would not have been punished by your betters and your equals would not now despise you."

Fine feathers do not make fine birds.

The Fox who lost his Tail

A FOX, having been caught in a trap, was able, after a severe struggle, to break away, but he was forced to leave his brush in order to save his neck. After a time he began to realize the disgrace which the loss of his tail would bring upon him, and he almost wished he had died in the trap.

At length, however, he made up his mind to put a good face on the matter. Calling a meeting of the foxes, he proposed that all should follow his example.

"You have no idea of the ease and comfort with which I now move about," said he; "I would never have believed it if I had not tried it myself; but really, when one comes to think of it, a tail is so inconvenient and unnecessary that it is a wonder that we should have put up with it so long."

He paused for a moment in the hope that he might find some support from his listeners, but as no one seemed inclined to interrupt, he continued:

"I propose, my worthy brethren, that you profit by the experience that I most happily possess, and that henceforth from this day all foxes cut off their tails."

An old fox, who had listened carefully to the suggestion, now stepped forward. "I rather think," he said, "that you would not have advised us to part with our tails if there had been any chance of recovering your own."

Beware of the counsel of the unfortunate.

The Dog invited to Supper

A GENTLEMAN prepared a feast and invited a friend to supper. His dog, chancing to meet the guest's dog, said: "Come and sup with us to-night, my good fellow."

The dog was delighted with the invitation, and as he stood by and saw the preparations for the feast said to himself, "This is indeed capital fare. I shall just revel in the dainties, and will take good care to eat all that I can to-night, for to-morrow I may go hungry."

As he said this the dog wagged his tail and gave a sly look at his friend. Unfortunately for him his wagging tail caught the cook's eye, and

he, seeing a strange dog in his kitchen, seized him by the tail and threw him out of the window.

When he reached the ground he ran yelping down the street, and the neighbours' dogs, hearing his cries, hastened to ask how he had enjoyed his supper.

"I hardly know," said the poor animal with

a sorry smile, "for we drank so deeply that I cannot even tell you which way I left the house."

They who enter by the back stairs may expect to be shown out at the window.

The Lion and the Mouse

A LION was sleeping in his lair when a mouse, not knowing where he was going, ran over the nose of the mighty beast and awakened him.

The lion put his paw upon the frightened little creature and was about to make an end of him, when the mouse, in a pitiful voice, said, "Spare me, I pray you, for I had lost my way and was so scared that I did not know what I was doing. Do not stain your honourable paws with so tiny a creature as me."

The fright of his little captive put the lion into a good humour and he generously let him go.

Now it happened soon after that the lion, while hunting in the woods, fell into a trap set for him, and finding himself entangled beyond hope of escape, he set up a roar that filled the forest with its echo.

The mouse, recognizing the voice of his former captor, ran to the spot and, without wasting a moment, set to work to nibble the knot in the cord that held the lion.

His teeth were sharp, and so it was not long before the noble beast was once more at liberty, wiser by the knowledge that the most lowly creature may have it in his power to return a kindness.

An act of kindness is a good investment.

The Fatal Marriage

THE lion, freed from the snare, was exceedingly grateful to the little mouse which had helped him, and made up his mind to reward him handsomely. He therefore asked the mouse what he would like, and the little creature, full of ambition and determined to make the most of his chance, asked for the lion's daughter as a wife. The lion agreed at once, and called his daughter to come to her husband. The young lioness came bounding along, and, not expecting her future husband to be so small or near the ground, accidentally set her foot on him and crushed him as he was running to meet her.

We should practise moderation in our requests, and not seek to have more than is good for us.

The Flies and the Honey-pot

A SWARM of flies came round a pot of honey which had been upset in a grocer's shop, nor would they leave the spot while there was a drop

left. After a time the honey stuck to their feet and wings so that they could not fly away. Then they cried, "What silly creatures we were! For the sake of a short hour's pleasure we have thrown away our lives!"

The greedy never know when they have
had enough.

The Ant and the Dove

AN ant went to a fountain to quench his thirst, but in so doing tumbled in and was almost drowned. A dove happened to be sitting on a neighbouring tree, and saw the ant's danger; plucking off a leaf, she let it drop into the water before the ant, and the tiny creature, mounting upon it, was presently carried safely to the side.

A little later a fowler was just about to cast his net over the dove, when the ant, seeing his friend's danger, bit the fowler's heel. The start which the man gave made him drop the net, and the dove, warned of her danger, flew safely away.

One good turn deserves another.

King Log and King Stork

A NUMBER of frogs lived a free and easy life among the ponds and lakes; after a time they tired of their mode of living and became thoroughly dissatisfied with their lot. They therefore met together one day and noisily demanded of Jupiter that he should give them a king who would govern them and make them live more useful lives.

It happened that Jupiter was in a good humour at the time, and he laughed heartily at their request.

Throwing a little log into the pool, he cried, " There is a king for you."

The sudden splash made by its fall into the water at first terrified the frogs so much that they were afraid to come near the log; but in a short time, seeing that it lay without moving, they ventured to approach it, and when they found that it was not to be feared, they leaped upon it and were very soon regarding it with contempt.

Such a useless king did not please them, and so they soon sent again to Jupiter and asked that they might be given a ruler of stronger character.

Determined to teach the frogs a lesson, Jupiter

sent them a stork, who, without any ceremony, commenced to eat them up, one after another, as fast as he could.

In their sorry plight those who survived asked Mercury to plead with Jupiter on their behalf, that he would bless them with yet another king, or, if it pleased him better, restore them to their former state.

"No," said Jupiter, "since it was their own choice, let the obstinate wretches suffer the punishment due to their folly."

Let well alone.

The Fawn and her Mother

A FAWN one day said to her mother, " Mother, you are larger, faster, and have better wind than a dog, and surely are able to protect yourself. How is it that you are so afraid of the hounds?"

To this the hind sadly replied, "What you have said, my child, is only too true, and yet no sooner do I hear a dog bark than, somehow or other, my heels take me off as fast as they can carry me."

A coward cannot be urged into courage.

The Country Maid and her Milk-pail

A COUNTRY maid was walking along with a pail of milk on her head, planning what she would do with the money she was to receive for the milk.

"I shall increase my stock of eggs to three hundred," she said to herself. "Allowing for those that prove to be addled, and a few that are

61

certain to be destroyed by vermin, these eggs will produce at least two hundred and fifty chicks. The chickens will be fit to carry to market just at a time when poultry is always dear, so that by the new year I cannot fail to have enough money to purchase a new gown. It should be of a green material, for green is most becoming and suits me best. I will go to the fair, and all the young men will strive to have me for a partner, but I shall refuse them all with a toss of my head."

So pleased was she with the idea that she put the thought into action, whereupon the pail of milk tumbled from her head and all her plans vanished in a moment.

Do not count your chickens before they are hatched.

The Old Woman and her Maids

I⊤ was the practice of an old and thrifty widow to call her two maids to their work every morning at cock-crow.

The maids disliked this early rising, and determined to wring the cock's neck, for they thought that by waking their mistress so early he was the cause of their discomfort.

Their cleverness failed to relieve them, however, for the old lady, missing her usual alarum, and afraid of oversleeping herself, frequently mistook the time and roused the maids at midnight.

Too much cunning over-reaches itself.

The Leopard and the Three Bulls

A LEOPARD had spent much time watching three bulls in the hope that he would be able to seize them for his prey.

His chance would come when they separated, but they seemed to enjoy each other's company so much that wherever one went his companions were sure to follow.

Realizing that he must capture them singly if at all, the leopard began to spread evil reports of one to the other until he had created jealousy and distrust among them, so that they fed apart from each other.

No sooner did the leopard see that they avoided one another than he fell upon them in turn, and so made an easy prey of them all.

The quarrels of friends are the opportunities of their foes.

The Eagle and the Arrow

An archer, taking good aim at an eagle, sent an arrow through his body, wounding him beyond all hope of recovery.

As the poor bird lay dying upon the ground he saw that the arrow was tipped with his own feathers. "Alas," said he, "how sharp are the wounds made by weapons which we ourselves have winged!"

Misfortunes we bring upon ourselves are
doubly bitter.

The Ass and the Lap-dog

A man once had an ass and a lap-dog. The ass was tied up in the stable and had plenty of corn and hay to eat and was as well off as any ass could be.   The little dog sported and ran about, licked his master's hand, and fawned upon him at every opportunity in a very amusing way, so that he became a great favourite, and his master often took him upon his lap.

Now the ass had plenty of work to do; he carted wood all day and at night was made to take his turn at the mill.   This after a time made him discontented, and he became jealous of the lap-dog, which lived in such ease and luxury.

"I will imitate the dog's ways," said he one day, "and then perhaps my master will treat me in a like manner."

Breaking away from his stable, he rushed into the house, kicking about and prancing in a most ungainly fashion.   Before long he upset the dinner-table, which was spread with a meal, broke it in two, and smashed all the crockery.   Then, not content with the damage he had done, he jumped upon his master and pawed him with his rough-shod feet.

The servants, seeing their master in danger, thought it time to interfere.   Pulling the foolish animal away, they beat him so hard with sticks that he could not get up again.

"How I wish I had been satisfied with my lot," he said, as he lay dying, "instead of attempting to imitate one who was but a puppy after all!"

Do not try to do that which is not natural to you.

The Dog, the Cock, and the Fox

A DOG and a cock, having become very friendly, decided to set out on their travels together.

Nightfall found them in a forest, and so, having no better shelter, the cock flew up to the branch of a tree, while the dog dozed at the foot.

The night passed peacefully away, and as the new day dawned the cock began to crow, according to his custom.

A fox near by heard the clarion call, and thinking that by flattering words he would persuade the cock to come down from the tree, and so be enabled to make a meal of him, he drew near and cried in wheedling tones :

"Thou art a good little bird, and most useful to thy fellow creatures. Come down that we may sing our morning prayers and rejoice together."

"Come close to the foot of the tree, my good friend," the cock replied, "and tell the sacristan to toll the bell."

The fox approached closer, but instead of the sacristan he found the dog, who jumped out and in a moment seized the cunning beast and made an end of him.

They who lay traps for others are often caught by their own bait.

Hercules and the Carter

As a carter was carelessly driving his wagon along a country road the wheels sank so deeply into the mud that the oxen came to a standstill.

Without making the least effort of his own the man began to call upon Hercules for his assistance.

Angered at the stupidity of the fellow, Hercules bade him get up, whip his oxen, and assist them by laying his shoulder to the wheel, assuring him that Heaven only aids those who try to help themselves.

It is useless to expect our prayers to be heard if we do not strive as well as pray.

The Wanton Calf

A WANTON calf, who spent his time in play and idleness, chanced to meet an ox employed in drawing a plough, and he could not resist the temptation to jeer at him.

"What a poor drudge you are," said he, "to

bear that heavy yoke upon your neck, and to draw
the plough at your tail all day long, turning up the
ground for your master. You must be a dull
slave and can know no better, or you would not
do it. See what a happy life I lead! I go
just where I please, sometimes lying down in
the cool shade, sometimes frisking about in the
glorious sunshine, and, when I wish, quenching
my thirst in the clear, sweet brook."

The ox, quite unmoved, went on quietly and
steadily with his work, and, when evening came,
was unyoked and allowed to wander at his will.

Now the following day had been set aside
as a day of sacrifice to the gods, and a holiday
throughout the land had been proclaimed.

Early in the morning the calf was taken from
the field in which he was grazing, and delivered
into the hands of the priest. His head was
encircled with a garland of flowers, and he
was led, with much ceremony, to the altar of
sacrifice.

The ox, who had watched the preparations with
much interest, now drew near and whispered:

"Behold the end of your insolence. It was
for this purpose that you were suffered to live in

idleness and luxury ; and now, friend, whose condition is the better, yours or mine ?"

Those who lead an idle life are apt to scorn the
honest and diligent, but their end is often miserable.

The Lion, the Bear, and the Fox

A LION and a bear, in search of food, chanced to
find the warm carcass of a fawn by the wayside.

Neither would agree to share the prize with
the other, and so it was not very long before they
came to blows.

The struggle was so hard and they were so
evenly matched that at last both fell to the
ground sorely wounded and without the strength
to touch the prize for which they had fought so
furiously.

A fox coming by at that moment saw their
helpless condition, and slipped in and carried off
the booty.

"What silly creatures we are," cried the bear;
"we have been wasting our strength and injuring
one another, only to give a rogue a dinner!"

Discretion is the better part of valour.

The Trees and the Axe

A woodcutter once came into a forest and asked
the trees to give him a handle for his axe.

This seemed such a small request that the
principal trees readily agreed, and decided that
the man should take the wood from the homely
ash-tree.

No sooner had the woodcutter got what he
wanted, however, than he began to fell the trees
around him, not even respecting the noblest trees
in the wood.

The oak trembled, knowing that it would be
her turn very soon, and she whispered to the
cedar: "If we had not been so ready to sacrifice

our humble neighbour we might have been spared to stand for ages ourselves."

When the rich surrender the rights of the poor they endanger their own privileges.

The Lion and the Boar

ON a hot summer's day, when everything was suffering from the extreme heat, a lion and a boar came at the same time to a small fountain to quench their thirst. They immediately began to quarrel as to which should drink first, till at length it seemed that each was determined to fight to the death rather than to give way. They rushed together with great fury, but after a time paused in their strife to recover breath.

Looking up, they saw a flock of vultures hovering above them, waiting the moment to fall upon the unfortunate loser of the battle. At this they made up their quarrel, "For," said they, "it is far better that we should live as friends than die to provide food for the vultures."

Do not enter into danger for the profit of others.

The Travellers and the Bear

Two friends were travelling on the same road together when they came face to face with a bear.

One in great fear, and without a thought of his companion, climbed into a tree and hid himself.

The other, seeing that, single-handed, he was no match for Bruin, threw himself on the ground and feigned death, for he had heard that a bear will not touch a dead body.

The bear approached him, sniffing at his nose and ears, but the man, with great courage, held his breath and kept still, and at length the bear, supposing him to be dead, walked slowly away.

When Bruin was well out of sight the first traveller came down from his tree and asked his companion what it was that the bear had said to him, " For," said he, " I observed that he put his mouth very close to your ear."

"Why," replied the other, "it was no great secret. He only advised me not to keep company with those who, when they get into difficulty, leave their friends in the lurch."

Misfortune tests the sincerity of friends.

The Tortoise and the Eagle

A TORTOISE became dissatisfied with his lowly life when he saw so many birds enjoying themselves in the air.

" If I could only get up into the air, I could soar with the best of them," he thought.

One day an eagle came to rest on a rock

beside him, and, seizing such a favourable opportunity, the tortoise offered all the treasures of the sea if only the monarch of the air would teach him to fly.

The eagle at first declined the task, for he considered it not only absurd but impossible, but, being further pressed by the entreaties and promises of the tortoise, he at length consented to do his best.

Taking him to a great height in the air, he loosed his hold, bidding the stupid creature to fly if he could.

Before the tortoise could express a word of thanks he fell upon a huge rock and was dashed to pieces.

The over-ambitious often destroy themselves.

The Monkey and the Camel

WHILE a meeting of the beasts was in progress a monkey greatly distinguished himself by dancing in a most entertaining manner, and was applauded by all present.

Moved by jealousy a camel came forward and

Hercules and the Carter

Page 68

The Tortoise and the Eagle

Page 75

began to dance also, but he made himself so utterly absurd that the beasts set upon him in indignation and drove him out of the ring.

Do not attempt to stretch your arm farther than your sleeve will allow.

The Horse and the Stag

A HORSE was pastured upon a wide meadow, which he had all to himself until a stag broke in and trod down the grass. This greatly annoyed the horse, which appealed to a man for help in punishing the intruder.

"Yes," said the man. "I will help you to be revenged upon the stag; but first you must let me put a bit in your mouth and mount upon your back. I will provide weapons."

The horse readily agreed, and together they chased and overcame the stag. Very pleased

77

with his revenge, the horse began to thank the man for his aid, but he received answer:

"No, do not thank me. I did not know until now how useful you could be to me. I should thank you, for henceforth I will keep you for my servant." Thus from that time the horse has been the slave of man.

Revenge is dearly bought at the price of liberty.

The Countryman and the Snake

A COUNTRYMAN, returning home one winter's day, found a snake lying by the hedge-side half dead with the cold.

Taking compassion on the creature, he carried it home to his fireside.

As soon as the warmth had revived it the

snake began to attack the children of the cottage, seeing which the countryman took up a mattock and put the treacherous creature to death.

Those who return evil for good may expect no pity.

The Thief and his Mother

A BOY once stole a book from one of his schoolfellows and brought it home to his mother, who instead of punishing him, as was her duty, gave him encouragement.

Many years passed, and the boy grew into a man; alas! he began to steal things of greater value, and at length was caught in the very act and sentenced to be hanged.

As he was being led away from the judge he saw his mother in the crowd that was following, and begged his jailers to allow him to speak to her.

Having obtained leave, he bent forward as if to whisper, but instead, he bit the lobe of her ear.

The pain made the old woman shriek, and the crowd cried out against her unnatural son, saying:

"Have you not been wicked enough already? Shame on you that your last deed should be one of cruelty to your mother!"

"Not so," replied the son, "my mother is the cause of my ruin, for had she flogged me when I brought a stolen book to her, as a boy, I should not have lived the life of wickedness that has brought me to this terrible end."

Spare the rod and spoil the child.

The Oxen and the Butchers

A NUMBER of oxen once determined to make an end of the butcher, whose whole art, they said, was directed to their destruction.

Waiting for a favourable opportunity, they assembled together with sharpened horns ready for the contest.

"Have a care what you do, my friends," said a very old ox. "These men at least kill us with decency and skill, but if we fall into unskilled hands we shall suffer a double death, for you may be well assured that men will not go without beef, even though they are without butchers."

It is better to bear the ills we have than to fly to others that we know not of.

The Kite, the Frog, and the Mouse

THERE was once much argument between a frog and a mouse as to which should be master of the fen, and many pitched battles resulted.

The crafty mouse, hiding under the grass, would make sudden sallies upon his enemy, often surprising him at a disadvantage.

The frog was stronger than his rival, however, and, hoping to end the dispute once for all, challenged the mouse to single combat.

The mouse accepted the challenge, and on the appointed day the champions entered the field, each armed with the point of a bulrush, and both confident of success.

A kite chanced to be hovering overhead at the time, and seeing the silly creatures so intent upon their quarrel she swooped suddenly down, seized them in her talons, and carried them off to her young.

People who wrangle and fight give opportunities to their enemies.

The Crab and his Mother

"Why do you walk in such a crooked way, my child?" said an old crab to her son. "You must learn to walk straight."

"Show me the way, mother," replied the young crab, "and when I see you taking a straight course I will try to follow."

Example is better than precept.

The Charger and the Ass

A CHARGER, beautifully groomed and equipped, one day came galloping along a road, exciting the envy of a poor ass who was trudging along in

84

the same direction with a heavy load upon his back.

"Get out of my way!" cried the proud horse, "or I shall trample you under my feet."

The ass said nothing, but quietly moved to one side of the road.

Not long afterward the charger went to the wars, and was badly wounded on the battlefield. Unfit for any further military service, he was sent home to work on the farm.

When the ass saw him painfully dragging a heavy wagon, "Ah!" said he to himself, "I need not have envied him in his pride; but for that he would not now lack a friend to help him in his need."

He who despises a humble friend may be doing
an ill turn to himself.

The Lamb and the Wolf

A LAMB pursued by a wolf took refuge in a temple, hoping that his enemy would not follow him there.

Hesitating at the door, the wolf called to him and said :

"The priest will slay you if he finds you in the temple, for he will say that you have been sent for a sacrifice."

"That may be so," replied the lamb, "but it is better to be slain at the altar than to be devoured by you."

Choose the lesser of two evils.

The Pig and the Sheep

A YOUNG pig took up his quarters in a fold with the sheep, and enjoyed the same life and privileges.

One day the shepherd laid hold of him, at which he squeaked and struggled with all his might and main.

The sheep reproached him for crying out, and said: "The master often lays hold of us and we do not cry."

"Yes," replied the pig, "but the case is somewhat different, for he catches you for the sake of your wool, but me for my flesh."

It is easy to cry " Coward! " when you are not in danger yourself.

The Miller, his Son, and their Ass

A MILLER and his son were driving their ass to a neighbouring fair to sell him.

They had not gone far when they met a troop of girls returning from the town, talking and laughing.

"Look there!" cried one of them; "did you ever see such fools, to be trudging along the road on foot, when they might be riding!"

The old man, hearing this, quietly bade his son get on the ass, and walked along merrily by the side of him. Presently they came to a group of old men, who were conversing together.

"There!" said one of them, "it proves what I was saying. What respect is shown to old age in these days? Do you see that idle young rogue riding while his old father has to walk?"

"Get down, you scapegrace, and let the old man rest his weary limbs!" cried another.

Upon this the father made his son dismount and got up himself; but they had not proceeded far when they met a company of women and children.

"Why, you lazy old fellow!" cried several tongues at once, "how can you ride upon the beast while this poor little lad can hardly keep pace by the side of you?"

The good-natured miller immediately took up his son behind him, and they rode in this manner until they had almost reached the town.

"Pray, honest friend," said a townsman, "is that ass your own?"

"Yes," replied the old man.

"By the way you load him, one would not have thought so," said the other. "Why, you two fellows are better able to carry the poor beast than he you!"

"If you think it the right thing to do," said the old man, "we can but try."

So, alighting with his son, they tied the ass's

legs to a stout pole, which they shouldered, and so got ready to carry him over a bridge that led to the town.

This was so entertaining a sight that the people ran out in crowds to laugh at it, until the ass, not liking the noise nor the situation, broke from the cords that bound him and tumbled off the pole into the river below.

Vexed and ashamed, the old man made the best of his way home again, convinced that by endeavouring to please everybody he had pleased nobody, and lost his ass into the bargain.

He who tries to please everybody pleases nobody.

The Fox and the Stork

A FOX one day invited a stork to dinner, and amused himself, at the expense of his guest, by providing nothing for the entertainment but some thin soup in a shallow dish.

This the fox lapped up very quickly, while the stork, unable to gain a mouthful with her long, narrow bill, was as hungry at the end of the dinner as when she began.

The fox expressed his regret at seeing her eat so sparingly, and feared that the dish was not seasoned to her liking.

The stork said little, but begged that the fox would do her the honour of returning the visit next day, which invitation Reynard readily accepted.

The fox kept the appointment, and, having greeted his hostess, turned his attention to the dinner placed before them.

To his dismay Reynard saw that the repast was served in a narrow-necked vessel, and, while the stork was able to thrust in her long bill and take her fill, he was obliged to content himself with licking the outside of the jar.

Unable to satisfy his hunger, he retired with as good grace as he could, knowing that he could hardly find fault with his hostess, for she had only paid him back in his own coin.

Those who love practical jokes must be prepared to laugh when one is made at their expense.

The Mole and her Mother

A YOUNG mole said one day to her mother, " Mother, I can see."

In order to test the truth of this statement the mother placed a piece of frankincense before her child and asked her what it was.

"A stone," eagerly replied the little mole.

"Oh, my child," said the mother, "not only are you blind, but it is evident that you have lost the sense of smell in addition."

Do not lay claim to a virtue you do not possess if you would keep the respect of your friends.

The Cat and the Fox

A CAT and a fox were exchanging views upon the difficulties of living in peace and safety from those who were ever ready to take their lives.

"I do not care a jot for any of them," said the fox at last. "Things may be very bad, as you say, but I have a thousand tricks to show my enemies before they can do me harm."

"You are fortunate," replied the cat. "For my part, I have but one way of evading my enemies, and if that fails all is lost."

"I am sorry for you with all my heart," said Reynard. "But that one cannot tell a friend from a foe in these difficult times, I would show you one or two of *my* tricks."

Hardly had he finished speaking when a pack of hounds burst suddenly upon them.

The cat, resorting to her single trick, ran up a tree, and from the security of the topmost branches witnessed the downfall of the braggart.

Unable to make up his mind which of the thousand tricks he would adopt, the fox was torn to pieces before he could put even one of them into operation.

He who considers himself more clever than his neighbour usually fares badly when put to the test.

The Bees, the Drones, and the Wasp

SOME bees built a comb in the hollow trunk of an oak-tree, but some drones claimed that they had built it, and that it belonged to them.

The case was brought into court before Judge Wasp, who, knowing something of the habits of both parties, addressed them thus:

"The plaintiffs and defendants are so much alike in shape and colour that it is difficult to say which are the rightful owners, and the case has very properly been brought before me. Now I think that justice will best be served by following out the plan which I propose. Let each party take a hive and build up a new comb, so that from the shape of the cells and the taste of the honey it will be quite clear to whom the comb in dispute belongs."

The bees readily agreed to the wasp's plan, but the drones, on the other hand, would not do so.

Whereupon the wasp gave judgment: "It is clear now who made the comb, and who cannot make it; the court gives judgment in favour of the bees."

We may know a tree by its fruit.

The Wolf and the Shepherd

A WOLF once followed a flock of sheep for a long time, and did not attempt to injure any of them. The shepherd at first was watchful of his movements and regarded him as an enemy, but when he saw that the wolf kept near the sheep but never harmed them he began to look upon him as a guardian of the flock instead of suspecting him of evil.   One day he was obliged to go to the town, and left his sheep to the charge of the wolf. This was the chance the wolf had been waiting for, and he fell upon the flock and destroyed the greater part of it.   The shepherd on his return, finding the dead bodies of many sheep, cried:

"It serves me right for trusting my flock to a wolf."

There is more danger from a pretended friend than from an open enemy.

The Eagle and the Beetle

A HARE pursued by an eagle took refuge in the nest of a beetle, whom he begged to save him. The beetle, therefore, asked the eagle not to kill the poor trembling animal and break the laws of hospitality just because a beetle was a tiny creature.

But the eagle gave the beetle a flap with her wing and flew off with the hare.

The beetle flew after her to see where her nest was, and, when the eagle was away, he rolled the bird's eggs out of it, one by one, and broke them. The angry eagle built her nest in a higher place, but the beetle discovered it, and treated the eggs in the same way as before.

Then the eagle, determined to find a safe place, flew up to the skies and laid her eggs in Jupiter's lap, begging him to take care of them.

The beetle now made a little ball of dirt and dropped it in Jupiter's lap, who, when he saw it, forgetting the eggs, rose up to shake it off, so that they were again broken.

When the beetle explained that he had done this because the eagle had ignored the little creature's plea, Jupiter upheld the beetle and told the eagle she had thoroughly deserved her punishment. But, as he did not wish eagles to die out altogether, he decreed that in future she should lay her eggs at another season, when there are no beetles to be seen.

Even the strongest may be punished when they oppress the weak.

The Eagle and the Jackdaw

An eagle, taking a favourable opportunity, swooped down from a high rock and carried off a lamb in his talons.

A jackdaw witnessed the exploit, and, thinking that he could do the like, bore down upon a ram with all the force he could muster.

But his claws became entangled in the wool, and in his efforts to escape he made such a commotion that he attracted the attention of the shepherd, who, seeing what was going on, came up and caught him, and, having clipped his wings, carried the foolish bird home to his children.

"What bird is this that you have brought us, Father?" asked the children.

"Why," replied the shepherd, "if you ask him he will tell you that he is an eagle, but if you will take my word for it he is only a very stupid jackdaw."

Those who, out of vanity, attempt more than they can perform are certain to bring ridicule upon themselves.

The Mule

A MULE, grown fat and care-free with good feeding, commenced one day to jump and gambol about, until she became thoroughly convinced that for speed and agility she was without rival.

"My mother was a race-horse," she cried, "and I can run quite as fast as she could!"

The exertion had such an effect upon her, however, that she very soon became thoroughly exhausted, and it was then that she remembered that her father was only a donkey.

There are two sides to every truth.

The House-dog and the Wolf

A LEAN, hungry wolf chanced one night to fall in with a plump, well-fed house-dog.

"How is it, my friend," said the wolf, "that

you look so well? It seems that you are able to obtain a plentiful supply of food, while I strive night and day for a living and can hardly save myself from starvation."

"If you would fare like me," replied the dog, "you have only to do as I do."

"Indeed!" said the other, "and what is that?"

"I guard the master's house at night and keep off thieves," was the reply.

"If that is all, I will throw in my lot with you with all my heart; for at present I have a sorry time of it prowling around in the frost and the rain without so much as a shelter for my weary bones. To have a warm roof over my head and a stomach full of good, wholesome food will, methinks, be no bad exchange."

Now as they were jogging along together the wolf spied the collar on the dog's neck, and, feeling curious, could not resist asking what it meant.

Pressed for an answer, the dog replied that it was only the collar to which his chain was fastened.

"Chain," cried the wolf in dismay; "you don't mean to say that you cannot rove when and where you please?"

"Well, not exactly perhaps," said his companion. "You see, I am looked upon as rather fierce, so they sometimes tie me up in the daytime. But at night I have perfect liberty; my master feeds me off his own plate, and the servants give me choice morsels. I am a great favourite and— but what is the matter? Where are you going?"

"Oh, good night to you," said the wolf. "You are welcome to your dainties, but for me a dry crust with liberty is better than a king's luxury with a chain."

Slavery is too high a price to pay for
easy living.

The Thief and the Yard Dog

A THIEF climbed the wall of a yard with the intention of robbing the house to which it belonged. When he saw the yard dog he threw him some pieces of meat to stop him barking, but the dog only barked the more.

"Off with you," he cried. "I suspected you when I first saw you, and now you are trying to stop my mouth I *know* you are a rascal."

A bribe in the hand shows mischief in the heart.

The Nurse and the Wolf

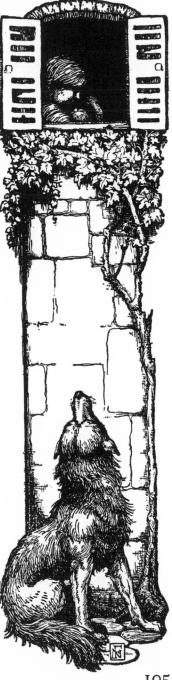

A NURSE, in the endeavour to quiet a wilful child, threatened to throw it out of doors to the wolf if it did not leave off crying.

A wolf chanced to be prowling near the door just then and heard what was said. Believing the woman to be in earnest, he waited outside the house for a long time in the hope that she would carry out her threat.

At last the child, wearied with so much crying, fell asleep, and the wolf was forced to return to the woods empty and supperless.

A fox, noticing his downcast appearance, asked the cause of his depression.

"Ah! do not ask me," replied the wolf. "I was silly enough to believe what a woman said, and have been disappointed."

It is not always wise to take people at their word.

The Man and his Two Wives

MANY years ago, when a man was allowed to have more than one wife, a bachelor, who could be called neither young nor old, and whose hair was only just beginning to turn grey, fell in love with two women at the same time and married them both.

One was young and pretty, and wanted her husband to look as youthful as herself; but the other was much older, and was just as anxious that he should look as old as herself.

So while the young wife seized every opportunity of pulling out her husband's grey hairs, the elder one was busy taking out every black hair she could find.

For some time the man was very pleased with their attention and devotion, until one morning he found that between the two of them he had not one hair left.

He who always gives way to others will end in having no principles of his own.

The Bull and the Goat

A BULL pursued by a lion took refuge in a cave where a wild goat lived. The goat began to worry the bull and butt at him with his horns.

"Butt away," said the bull; "I am not afraid of you, but of the lion outside. When he has gone I will soon show you the difference between a bull and a goat."

Men who take advantage of their neighbours'
difficulties to annoy them will repent
later of their insolence.

The Lark and her Young Ones

A LARK had made her nest in a field of corn, and when it was ripe the mother lark, looking every day for the reapers, told her young ones to report all the news they heard while she was away looking for food.

One day she returned and found her nestlings in a great state of excitement. "Mother, Mother," they cried, "we must go at once. The farmer and his son have been here, and the farmer said that to-morrow he should get his neighbours to help him cut the corn."

"His neighbours!" said

The Fox and the Crow

Page 110

The Fox and the Grapes

Page 127

the mother lark. "Oh, there is time enough yet if he trusts to his neighbours to get his harvest in for him."

The next day she was again greeted by excited pipings. "Mother, Mother, we must fly away at once," the young ones cried; "the farmer says

he is going to get his *relations* to cut the corn. His son has gone to call their uncles and cousins to come to-morrow."

"Don't be frightened," said the mother lark, "his relations have harvest work of their own to do. Your wings will be stronger for another day's rest. Listen well, and tell me what you hear."

The next day on her return to the nest the young ones cried, "The farmer has been here again. He says he and his son will cut the corn themselves to-morrow as his relations and his neighbours have failed him."

"In that case," said their mother, "early to-morrow morning we will fly away, for when a man says he will do a thing *himself* it generally gets done."

Self-help is the best help.

The Fox and the Crow

A CROW snatched a piece of cheese from a window and flew with it to a tree, intent on enjoying her prize. A fox spied her with the dainty morsel, and stood beneath the branch on which she sat.

"O crow," he said, "what beautiful wings you have, and what bright eyes! What a graceful neck is yours, and the plumage of your breast is like an eagle's! Surely your voice must equal your beauty. Pray sing to me and let me hear for myself." The crow, pleased with the flattery, opened her mouth to give a loud caw—and down fell the cheese!

The fox snapped up the dainty morsel, and remarked, as he walked away: "Whatever I have said of her beauty, I will make no remarks concerning her brains!"

Beware of flatterers.

The Lioness

THERE was much talk among the animals as to which of them could boast of the largest family.

They decided to settle the matter by sending messengers through the length and breadth of the country to ask all mothers how many children they had at one time.

Before the messengers had gone very far they

came to the lair of a lioness. "And how many cubs do you have at a birth?" they asked.

"One," she grimly replied; "but that one is a lion."

Quality is better than quantity.

The Goose with the Golden Eggs

A CERTAIN man had the good fortune to possess a goose that laid a golden egg every day.

Dissatisfied with one egg a day, and thinking to obtain the whole treasure at once, he killed the goose, and, cutting her open, found her—just what any other goose would be!

Let well alone.

The Lion and his Three Counsellors

A LION called a sheep to him and asked her if his breath smelt.

"Yes," she replied, and he killed her for her foolishness.

He then called a wolf and asked the same question.

"No, not at all," replied the wolf; but he fared no better, for the lion tore him to pieces, calling him a flatterer.

Finally the lion asked a fox his opinion on the matter.

113

"I have a bad cold," crafty Reynard replied, "and can smell nothing at all."

Wise men keep a guard on their tongues.

The Ass and the Grasshopper

AN ass was browsing on the tender grass of a meadow when he was greatly attracted by the chirping of some grasshoppers. It occurred to him that he also would like to make such enchanting sounds, and he asked the little creatures to tell him what sort of food they ate, for he thought that it must be their food which gave them such melodious voices. The grasshoppers replied, "The dew"; whereupon the ass resolved to live only upon dew. In a short time he died of hunger.

One man's meat is another man's poison.

The Wolf and the Goat

A WOLF saw a young goat feeding on the top of a high cliff where he had no chance of reaching him. He called up to the goat: "You had better be careful or you may miss your footing! Do come down here; the grass is much sweeter, and there is more of it."

"Thank you," said the goat, "but I do very well here, and if I came down to you, it is you who would feed better, not I."

The advice of an enemy is not to be trusted.

The Oak and the Reeds

An oak which hung over a river was uprooted by a violent storm of wind and carried down the stream. As it floated along it noticed some reeds growing by the bank, and cried out to them,

"Why, how do such slight, frail things as yourselves manage to stand safely in a storm which can tear *me* up by the roots?"

"It was easy enough," answered the reeds; "instead of standing stubbornly and stiffly against it as you did, we yielded and bowed before every wind that blew, and so it went over us and left us unhurt."

It is better to bend than to break.

The Angler and the Little Fish

An angler, who gained his livelihood by his fishing, toiled the day long and caught but one little fish.

"Spare me, I beseech you," said the little creature; "I shall make you but a sorry meal, for I have not yet come to my full size. Throw me back into the river, and when I am bigger and worth eating you may come here and catch me again."

"No, no," replied the fisherman; "I have got you now, but if you get back into the water your tune will be, 'Catch me if you can.'"

A bird in the hand is worth two in the bush.

The Sick Wolf and the Lamb

A WOLF that was sick and unable to move called to a lamb that was passing by and begged her to fetch him some water from a neighbouring stream.

"If you will bring me drink," said he, "I will manage to find the meat for myself."

"I daresay you will," said the lamb, backing away cautiously. "For if I come near enough to bring you the drink I know very well that I shall provide the meat as well."

Beware of hypocrites.

The Mouse and the Weasel

A LITTLE starved mouse had made his way with some difficulty into a basket of corn, where he stuffed and crammed himself to such an extent that when he wanted to get out again he found the hole too small to allow his puffed-up body to pass. As he struggled to squeeze through a weasel, who was attracted to the spot by his cries, said to him: "Stop there, my friend, and fast till you are thin again; for you will never come out till you are reduced to the same condition as when you entered."

The remedy may be as bad as the disease.

The Quack Frog

A FROG, who was tired of life in a marsh, hopped out of his swamp and made a proclamation to all the beasts that he was a wonderful doctor and could heal all the diseases in the world.

The animals flocked round him as he waved his medicine bottle. "Here," he cried, "is a wonderful drug. There is nothing it will not cure." Then up came a fox. "Who are you," cried the fox, "to pretend to cure all things while you go limping through the world with bandy legs, a wrinkled skin, and goggle eyes?"

Physicians should first heal themselves.

The Farmer and the Dogs

DURING a very severe winter a farmer was snowed up in his farmhouse. Before many days had passed he had consumed all the food in his store, and, being unable to get to the town to replenish his stock, was forced to kill his own sheep to keep his family from starvation.

Day followed day, and still there was no break in the weather, wherefore, having killed the last of his sheep, the farmer sorrowfully turned to his goats, taking them for food as the need arose.

Weeks passed, and still the terrible weather held. The poor farmer had come to the end of his goats, and, having no other food, was forced to kill the first of his plough-oxen.

Seeing this the dogs said to one another: "Let us be off; for, since the master has had no pity on the working oxen, it is hardly likely that he will spare us."

When our neighbour's house is on fire it is time to look to our own.

The Wolf in Sheep's Clothing

A WOLF once found a sheep's skin, and, thinking he would have an easy way of getting his prey, wrapped himself in it and slipped into the sheep-fold with the flock, intending to kill all he wanted during the night. But soon after the shepherd had made the door fast he found he had nothing for supper, and, going in with an axe to kill a sheep, he mistook the wolf for one of them and killed him on the spot.

The wicked often fall into their own snares.

The Ass in the Lion's Skin

An ass, having found a lion's skin in the forest, put it on, and, pretending to be the King of the Beasts, amused himself by frightening the foolish animals he met in his wanderings. Before he had gone far he met a fox, and tried to frighten him also.

"When I hear a lion roar I am alarmed," remarked the fox, "but when he brays, whatever coat he wears, I know him to be only an ass."

Clothes do not make the man.

The Stag at the Pool

A STAG one hot summer day came to a clear pool to drink, and as he did so he saw himself reflected in the water and stayed for some time looking at the reflection.

"What beautiful horns I have," he said; "how strong they are, and how splendidly branched, and how handsome they look on my head! If only all my body were equally fine—

but I must say these slender legs of mine make me feel quite ashamed when I look at them, they are so thin and unsuitable."

At that moment he heard the sound of the huntsman's horn and the baying of the hounds. The legs he had so despised carried him nimbly across a plain, and he soon left men and dogs behind; but at last he ran into a dense wood, and the horns, of which he was so proud, became entangled in a thicket and held him till the hunters came up, and the dogs pulled him down.

Use is better than ornament.

The Widow and the Hen

A WIDOW who kept a hen that laid an egg every morning once thought to herself:

"If I double my hen's allowance of barley, she will lay twice each day."

So she tried her plan, and the hen became so fat and lazy that she left off laying altogether.

Figures are not always facts.

The Wolf and the Lion

A HUNGRY wolf had seized a sheep from a fold and was dragging it home to his den when he met a lion, who straightway laid hold of the sheep and began to carry it away.

"What a shame," snarled the wolf, "to rob me of what was mine!"

"Your own, was it?" sneered the lion. "Your friend the shepherd gave it to you, I suppose!"

They who live by robbery cannot call other men thieves.

The Horse and the Lion

A HUNGRY lion, seeing a plump horse which he thought would make a good meal, drew near with the intention of pouncing upon him. But as he knew the horse could easily outdistance him if it came to a race, he called out in a friendly voice, and said that he was a great physician and could cure all ills. The horse guessed his evil intention and made up his mind to be even with him, so he told the lion he had a thorn in his foot and begged him to examine it. He lifted up one of his hind legs, and, as the lion pretended to peer at it, gave him such a kick in the face that the lion went sprawling on the ground, quite stunned. Then the horse trotted away, laughing at the success of his trick upon one who meant to deprive him of his life by cunning.

Those who lay snares for others may fall victim to their own wiles.

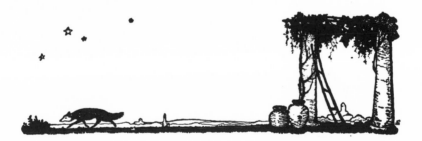

The Fox and the Grapes

A FOX, feeling very hungry, made his way to a vineyard near by, where he knew he would find a plentiful supply of grapes.

The season had been a good one, and he licked his lips when he saw the huge bunches hanging from the vine.

His joy was short-lived, however, for, try as he would, the grapes were just out of his reach.

At last, tired by his vain efforts, he turned away in disgust, remarking: "Anyone who wants them may have them for me. They are too green and sour for my palate; I would not touch them even if they were given to me."

It is a mean nature which affects to dislike that which it is unable to obtain.

The Hedge and the Vineyard

A FOOLISH young man, having come into possession of his father's estate, caused the hedges about his vineyard to be burned because they bore no grapes.

Thus his grounds were laid open to the ravages of man and beast, and before long his vines were destroyed.

In this way the simple fellow learnt, but when it was too late, that it is idle to expect to gather grapes from brambles, and that he who would possess a vineyard must protect it.

There is a use for everything.

The Wild Boar and the Fox

A WILD boar was sharpening his tusks against a tree when a fox came up and asked him why he did so. "I can see no reason for it," he cried; "there are no hunters near, nor any hounds, nor any other danger that I can see."

"No," replied the boar, "but when danger

comes I shall have something else to do than sharpen my tusks."

It is too late to prepare for danger when
our enemies are upon us.

The Fox and the Woodman

A FOX pressed hard by hounds came to a man who was cutting wood, and begged to be shown a place of safety. Some bundles of faggots were close at hand, and the man allowed the fox to creep behind them.

Not many minutes later the hunters came up and asked the woodman if he had seen the fox.

"No," he replied, but pointed his thumb to the corner where the animal lay hid.

The hunters did not understand the hint, however, and went off again immediately. When they were out of sight the fox began to steal silently away, seeing which the man scolded him, saying: "Is this the way you take leave of your host, without so much as a word of thanks for your safety?"

"A pretty host!" said the fox, stopping to reply. "If you had been as loyal in your actions as your were with your tongue I should not have left you without a word of farewell."

There may be as much malice in a wink as in a word.

The Ass, the Cock, and the Lion

An ass and a cock were together in a farmyard when a lion entered, desperate from hunger. He was about to spring on the ass when the cock crowed loudly. A lion cannot bear the crowing of a cock, so giving up his purpose he fled away as fast as he could. Seeing him thus run away, the ass became bold and galloped after. When they had run some distance the lion, now far from the cock, turned about and tore the ass to pieces.

False confidence may lead us into danger.

The Creaking Wheels

As some oxen were dragging a wagon along a very heavy bit of road the wheels set up a tremendous creaking. "Stop your noise!" cried the wagoner. "What have you to cry out for when they who are drawing all the weight are silent?"

Those who cry loudest are rarely the most hurt.

The Fox and the Mask

A FOX one night stole into the house of an actor, and in turning over his various properties came upon a fine mask. "It looks very well," he cried, "but what is the good of it without any brains?"

A fine appearance is a poor substitute for inward worth.

The Bear and the Fox

A BEAR was boasting one day of his great love for man, saying that he had such a respect for him that he would not even touch his dead body. A fox, hearing these words, said with a smile, " I should think more of your professions of love if you never ate him alive."

Kindness is better bestowed on the living than on the dead.

The Bat and the Weasels

A BAT fell to the ground and was captured by a weasel. Fearing that he would be killed, he begged the weasel to let him go.

"Alas," said the weasel, "I cannot let you go, for on principle I am the enemy of all birds."

"But I am not a bird at all, I am a mouse," the bat replied.

"Why so you are," said the weasel, "now that I come to look at you," and he let the bat go.

Several days later the bat was caught by another weasel just as he had been before, and he found himself pleading once again for his life.

"No," said the weasel, "I have never yet let a mouse go."

"But I am not a mouse," the bat said, "I am a bird."

"Why so you are," replied the weasel, and he too let the bat go.

Always see which way the wind blows before making a commitment.

The Lion, the Fox, and the Beasts

A LION once let it be known that he was dying, and he summoned the other animals to come and hear his will and testament. First a goat came to the lion's cave, and he stopped there to listen for a long time. Then a sheep arrived, and even before she could come out a calf stepped up to receive the last wishes of the king of the beasts. But soon the lion seemed to recover his strength, and coming to the entrance of his cave, he saw a fox, who had been waiting outside for some time.

"Why do you not come to pay your respects to me?" said the lion to the fox.

"I beg your pardon," said Reynard, "but I have observed the tracks of the other animals who have come to see you; and while I see many hoof-marks going in, I see that there are none coming out. Until the animals who have entered your cave come out again I believe I would prefer to remain outside."

It is easier to fall into the enemies' hands than to get out of them.

The Frogs' Complaint against the Sun

ONCE upon a time, when the sun had announced his intention to marry, the frogs raised their voices and shouted into the sky. Jupiter was most disturbed by the noise of their croaking, and he asked them to tell him the reason for their complaint. One brave frog spoke up, saying, "Even when the sun is single he dries out the marsh, and forces us to die miserably in our arid homes; what will become of us should he create other suns?"

Nature never breaks her own laws.

The Nightingale and the Swallow

A SWALLOW, conversing with a nightingale, advised her to leave the leafy grove where she had made her home, and to come and live with men, nesting under the shelter of their roofs, as she herself did. But the nightingale replied, "There was a time when I lived among men, as do you, but the memory of the cruelties that I suffered at their hands is so strong that never again will I come near their dwellings."

The scene of past suffering renews painful memories.

The Crow and the Raven

A CROW was extremely jealous of a raven because he was believed by men to fortell the future and accorded the great respect due a bird of omen. She was eager to obtain a similar reputation for herself, and one day, seeing travellers coming near, she flew to the branch of a tree near the roadside and cawed as loudly as she could. The travellers stood still in dismay, fearing the sound was a bad omen. Finally, one of them caught sight of the crow, and said to his companions, "My friends, we can now go on without fear, for it is only a crow and that means nothing."

Those who pretend to be something they are not only make themselves ridiculous.

The Hare with many Friends

A HARE was very popular among the other animals. One day she heard the hounds approaching and thought she would escape the danger with the help of her many friends. Going up to the horse, she asked him to take her away from the hounds on his back. But the horse declined, saying that he had more important work to do for his master. "I am sure," said he, "that your other friends will come to your assistance."

The hare then pleaded with the bull in the hopes that he would agree to repel the hounds with his horns. But the bull replied, "Truly I am sorry, I have an appointment with a lady, but I am certain that your friend the goat will be able to help."

The goat, however, feared that his back might harm her if he took her upon it. The ram, he felt sure, was the proper friend to ask. So off she went to the ram and pleaded her case. The ram replied, "Another time, dear friend. I do not care to interfere on this occasion, as hounds have been known to eat sheep as well as hares."

The hare then addressed herself to the calf, as a last hope, but he regretted that he was unable to help her, as he felt uneasy accepting this great responsibility when so many older animals had declined the task.

All at once the hare realized that the hounds were really quite near, and picking up her heels, she ran away, and luckily escaped.

He that has many friends has no friends.

The Horse and the Miller

A HORSE, feeling the weakness of his old age, found a position in the mill instead of on the battlefield. But when he was forced to grind corn instead of serving in the wars, he bitterly regretted his change of fortune, and recalled his former state of glory, saying, "Ah, miller, when I went to battle before, I was covered in shining armor and had a man along to groom me; now I cannot tell what ailed me to prefer the mill to the wars."

"Cease," said the miller to him, "from dwelling upon the past, for it is the common fate of men to bear the ups and downs of fortune."

It is an aspect of all happiness to suppose that we deserve it.

The Spendthrift and the Swallow

A SPENDTHRIFT, who had wasted his fortune and had nothing left to his name but the clothes on his back, spotted a swallow on a fine day in early spring. Thinking that summer had come, and that he would no longer need his coat, he went off and sold it for what little he could get. When the weather changed, as it often does in the spring, there came a bitter frost which killed the unfortunate swallow. When the spendthrift saw the dead bird he cried, "Miserable bird! Thanks to you I am dying of the cold."

One swallow does not make summer.

The Owl and the Birds

AN OWL, in her wisdom, counselled the birds that when the acorn first sprouted they should pull it from the earth and by no means allow it to grow, for, she said, it would produce mistletoe, from which men extract the deadly bird-lime they use to capture birds. The wise owl next advised the birds to pluck from the fields the flax seed that men had sown, as flax was a plant which could only harm them. Finally, seeing an archer approach, she predicted that men, from their lowly position on the ground, would invent arrows armed with feathers which would fly faster than the wings of the birds themselves. The birds paid small attention to her warnings, and believing the owl to be beside herself, they said, afterward, that she was mad. Still later, finding to their grief that her words had been true, they marveled at her knowledge and called her the wisest of all birds. So it is that when she appears they address her as one knowing all things, but she will no longer provide them with advice, and laments their foolishness alone.

The wise man does at once what the fool does finally.

The Hunter and the Woodman

A HUNTER, not being very bold, was searching in the forest for the tracks of a lion. He asked a woodman felling oaks if he had seen the prints of the lion's paws, or if indeed he knew where his lair was.

"I will, if you like, show you the lion himself," said the woodman. Turning pale and chattering his teeth with fear, the hunter replied, "No, thank you. I did not ask for that. It is his track alone I am in search of, and not the lion himself."

The hero is brave in deed as well as words.

The Bee Keeper

A THIEF once found his way into an apiary when the bee keeper was away, and stole all the honey. When the keeper returned to find the hives empty, he was quite upset and stood, stock still, staring at them for a time. Before too long the bees returned from gathering honey, and finding their hives overturned and the keeper standing by, they rushed upon him with their stings. At this the keeper angrily cried, "You ungrateful wretches, you let the thief who stole my honey get off free, and then you sting me, I who have always taken such good care of you!"

When you hit back make sure you have got the right man.

The Ants

THE ANTS were once men and made their living by tilling the soil. But, discontented with their own work, they were always coveting the fruits and crops of their neighbors, which they stole, whenever they had a chance, and added to their own stores. At last their greed made Jupiter so angry that he changed them into ants. But though their shapes were changed, their nature remained the same, and so, to this very day, the ants wander about the cornfields to gather the fruits of other men's labour, and store them up for their own use.

You may punish a thief, but his habits remain.

The Swan and the Goose

A CERTAIN very wealthy man bought in the market a goose and a swan. One he fed for his table, and the other he kept for the sake of its song. One night, when the time had come to kill the goose, the cook came to take it away, but in the dark he could not tell the two birds apart and caught the swan instead of the goose. The swan, threatened with death, burst forth with a song, and making himself known by his voice, he saved his own life with a melody.

A word in season is most precious.

The Eagle and the Fox

AN EAGLE and a fox became close friends, and decided to live near each other. The eagle built her nest in the branches of a tall tree, and the fox bore her young among the low bushes and thickets. Not long after they had agreed upon this plan, the fox was out searching for food, and the eagle, needing provisions, swooped down and seized one little fox to make a feast for herself and brood. The fox, on her return, grieved less for the death of her young than for her lack of a means of revenge.

A just retribution, however, quickly fell upon the eagle. While hovering near a fire where some villagers were cooking a goat, she suddenly seized a piece of meat, but with it carried to her nest a burning cinder. The strong wind blowing that day fanned the spark into a fire, and when the eagle pushed her young from the nest in the vain hope that they would fly, the fox ate them all up right in front of her.

Those who cause evil are the first to be
overwhelmed by its ruin.

The Peasant and the Apple Tree

A PEASANT had in his garden an apple tree, which bore no fruit, but served only to house sparrows and grasshoppers. He therefore resolved to cut it down, and taking up his axe, he struck boldly at its roots. The grasshoppers and sparrows pleaded with him, saying that if he would spare the tree they would sing to him and lighten his labours. The peasant, paying no attention to their cries, gave the tree another blow, but when he reached the hollow trunk he found a hive full of honey. Tasting the honeycomb, he threw down his axe, and vowed to take great care of the sacred tree.

Self interest alone moves some men.

The Wolf, the Fox, and the Ape

A WOLF once accused a fox of theft, but the fox fiercely denied the charge, holding that he was innocent of any wrong. An ape undertook to judge the matter, and when each party had fully stated his case, the ape pronounced this verdict: "I do not think you, O wolf, ever lost what you claim; and I do believe you, master Reynard, to have stolen what you so loudly deny."

The dishonest, if they act honestly, get no credit.

The Gnat and the Bull

A GNAT landed on the horn of a bull and sat there for a long time. Just as he was about to fly off, he made a buzzing noise and asked the bull if he would like him to go. The bull replied, "I did not know you had come, and I shall not miss you when you go away."

Some men are of more consequence in their own eyes than in those of their neighbours.

The Kites and the Swans

THE KITES, many years ago, possessed, equally with the swans, the remarkable privilege of song. But having once heard the neigh of a horse, they became so enchanted with the sound that they tried their best to imitate it, and so forgot how to sing.

A desire for imaginary benefits often involves the loss of present blessings.

The Cat and the Cock

A CAT pounced upon a cock, and was searching for some excuse to eat him, for cats don't usually make a meal of cocks, and she knew she ought not to. At last she said, "You, cock, make a great nuisance of yourself by crowing and keeping people awake, so I shall make an end of you."

But the cock defended himself, saying that he crowed so that men might awake and set about the day's work in the early hours of the morning, and that men could not very well do without him."

"That may well be," said the cat, "but whether they can or not, I am not going to go without dinner," and she ate him.

The want of a good excuse never kept a villain from crime.

The Peacock and the Crane

A PEACOCK, spreading out his gorgeous tail, mocked a crane that passed by, ridiculing the ashen hue of his feathers, and saying, "I am robed, like a king, in gold and purple, and all the colours of the rainbow, while you have not a trace of colour on your wings."

"True," replied the crane, "but I soar to the highest clouds and lift up my voice to the stars, while you must walk below, like a cock, among the birds of the dunghill."

Fine feathers do not make fine birds.

The Eagle and the Lion

AN EAGLE flew down from the sky, and begged a lion to make an alliance with him to their mutual advantage. The lion answered wisely, "I have no objection, but you must excuse me for requiring you to provide evidence of your good faith, for how can I trust any friend, who is able to fly away from his obligations whenever he pleases?"

Try before you trust.

The Cat and the Birds

A CAT heard that the birds in an aviary were ailing, so clothing himself as a doctor, and taking with him a set of the instruments proper to his profession, he presented himself at their door, and inquired after their health.

"We shall do very well," the birds responded, without letting him in, "when we have seen the last of you."

A villain may disguise himself, but he will not deceive the wise.

The Two Travellers and the Axe

Two men were travelling together in each other's company. One of them took up an axe that lay upon the path, and said, "I have found an axe."

"No, my friend," replied the other man, "do not say 'I', but 'We' have found an axe."

They had not walked much further before they noticed the owner of the axe pursuing them. The man who had picked up the axe said, "We are undone."

"No," replied the other, "keep to your first speech, my friend. What you thought right then, think right now. Say 'I,' not 'We' are undone."

He who shares the danger ought to share the prize.

The Thirsty Pigeon

A PIGEON, oppressed by excessive thirst, spotted a goblet of water painted on a signboard. Not believing it to be only a picture, she flew towards it with a loud whir, and unwittingly dashed against the signboard and jarred herself terribly. Breaking her wings by the blow, she fell straight to the ground, and was promptly caught by one of the bystanders

Zeal should not outrun discretion.

The Lamb Chased by a Wolf

A WOLF was pursuing a lamb, which took refuge in a nearby temple. The wolf urged it to come out of the precincts, and said, "If you don't leave the temple, the priest is sure to catch you and offer you up to on the altar to the gods."

To which remark the little lamb replied, "Thank you, I believe I will stay where I am, for I would rather be sacrificed any day than be eaten by a wolf."

Advice tempered by greed is best ignored.

The Farmer and the Fox

A FARMER was greatly annoyed by a fox, who came prowling about his yard at night and carried off many of his chickens. So he set a trap for him and caught him, and to have his revenge, he tied a bunch of tow to Reynard's tail, and set fire to it, and let him go. As luck would have it, however, the fox made straight for some fields where corn was standing ripe and ready for cutting. The corn quickly caught fire and burnt up, and the farmer lost all of his harvest.

Revenge is a two-edged sword.

The Serpent and the Eagle

AN EAGLE swooped down upon a poisonous serpent and seized him in his talons, intending to carry him off and devour him. But the serpent was too quick for him, and twisting his coils around the eagle, there ensued a deadly struggle between the two creatures. A countryman, witnessing the fight, came to the assistance of the eagle, and succeeding in freeing him from the serpent and enabled him to escape. In revenge the serpent spat some of his venom into the countryman's drinking-horn. Heated by his exertions, the man was about to quench his thirst with a long draught from the horn, when the eagle knocked it from his hand and spilled its contents upon the ground.

One good turn deserves another.

The Swallow and the Crow

THE SWALLOW and the crow had an argument about their plumage. It was the crow who put an end to their dispute by saying, "Your feathers are all very well in the spring, but mine protect me against the winter."

Fine feather friends are not worth much.

The Ass's Brains

A LION and a fox went out hunting together one day. The lion, taking the advice of the fox, sent a message to an ass, proposing to make an alliance between their two families. The ass arrived promptly at the place of meeting, overjoyed at the prospects of a royal alliance. But there the lion pounced on him and killed him, crying to the fox, "Here is our dinner for today. Keep watch here while I go and have a nap, and woe betide you if you touch my prey."

The fox waited for some time, but finding that his master did not return, ventured to take for himself the ass's brains, and made his meal. When the lion returned he soon noticed the absence of the brains, and said in a terrible voice, "What have you done with the brains?"

"Brains, your majesty?" said Reynard, "that ass had none or it would never have fallen into your trap."

Wit always has an answer ready.

The Dog and the Wolf

A DOG was lying asleep in the sun before a farmyard gate when a wolf caught him. Pleading for his life, the dog addressed the wolf with these words: "O wolf, you see how thin I am and what a wretched meal I should make you now, but if you will only wait a few days my master is going to give a feast. All the rich scraps and pickings will fall to me and I shall become nice and fat; then will be the time for you to eat me."

The wolf believed this to be a very good plan, and went away. Some time afterward he came to the farmyard again, and found the dog lying out of reach on the stable roof. "Come down," he called, "and be eaten, you remember our agreement?"

But the dog said coolly, "My friend, if ever you catch me lying down by the gate again, don't wait for any feast."

Once bitten, twice shy.

The Mountains in Labour

ONE day some countrymen noticed that the nearby mountains were in labour; smoke belched from their summits, the earth was quaking underfoot, trees crashed to the earth, and giant rocks tumbled from the hillsides. Certain that something horrible was about to occur, the men gathered together in one place to await what would happen. They waited and they waited, but nothing came. Finally the earth heaved and quivered with even more violence, and a huge gap appeared in the side of the mountains. The countrymen quickly fell upon their knees. At last, a teeny, tiny mouse poked his little head and whiskers out of the gap and came running down towards them.

Much outcry, little outcome.

The Peacock and Juno

A PEACOCK, desiring to have the voice of a nightingale in addition to all his other attractions, once placed a petition before Juno, but Juno refused his request. When he persisted, and pointed out that he was, after all, her favorite bird, she replied, "Be content with your lot; one cannot be first in everything.

No bird soars too high if he soars with his own wings.

The Lion and the Frog

A LION, hearing someone speaking in an odd sort of hollow voice, and seeing no one, stood up with a start. He listened again, and perceiving the voice to continue, trembled and quivered in fear. Finally, seeing a little frog crawl out of the lake, and discovering that all the terrible noise he had heard was nothing but the croakings of that tiny creature, he ran up to the frog, and killed him with a single blow of his paw.

Fear is often more dangerous than wrath.

160

The Huntsman and the Fisherman

A HUNTSMAN, returning with his dogs from the field, fell in by chance with a fisherman who was bringing home a basket well-laden with fish. The huntsman wished to obtain the fish, and their owner expressed an equal longing for the contents of the game-bag. The men quickly agreed to exchange the spoils of their day's sport. Each was so well pleased with his bargain, that they made the same exchange day after day for some time. A neighbour said to them, "If you go on in this way, you will soon destroy, by too frequent use, the pleasures of the exchange, and each will again wish to retain the fruits of his own sport."

Abstain and enjoy.

The Travellers and the Plane-Tree

Two TRAVELLERS, worn out by the heat of the summer's sun, laid themselves down at noon under the generous branches of a plane-tree. As they rested under the welcome shade, one of the travellers said to the other, "What a singularly useless tree is the plane! It bears no fruit, and is not of the least service to man."

The plane-tree, interrupting his speech, said, "O ungrateful men! Do you, while receiving benefits from me and resting so comfortably under my shade, dare to describe me as useless, and unprofitable?"

Some men despise their blessings.

The Oak and the Woodcutters

THE WOODCUTTERS chopped down a mountain oak and split it into pieces, making wedges of its own branches for dividing the trunk to save themselves the labour. The unfortunate oak said with a sigh, "I do not care about the blows of the axe aimed at my roots, but I do grieve at being torn into pieces by

these wedges made from my own branches."
*Misfortunes springing from ourselves are the
hardest to bear.*

The Ass and his Purchaser

A MAN wished to purchase an ass, and agreed with its owner that he should try him before he bought him. So he took the ass home, and putting him in the pasture with all his other asses, the man saw that the ass left the others, and joined himself in company with the most idle and the greatest eater of them all. The man promptly put a halter on the ass, and led him back to his owner; and on his inquiring how, in so short a time, he could have made a trial of him, the man replied, "I do not need a trial, for I know that he will be just such an ass as the one he chose for a companion from all the rest."

A man is known by the company he keeps.

The Wolf and the Horse

A WOLF coming out of a field of oats met up with a horse, and addressed him, saying, "I would advise you to go into that field. It is full of splendid oats,

163

which I have left untouched for you, as you are a friend the very sound of whose teeth it will be a pleasure for me to hear."

The horse responded, "If oats had been the food of wolves, you would never have indulged your ears at the cost of your belly."

Men of evil reputation, when they perform a good deed, fail to get credit for it.

The One-Eyed Doe

A DOE had had the misfortune to lose one of her eyes, and was unable to see anyone approaching her on that side. So as to avoid any danger, she became accustomed to feeding on a high cliff near the sea, with her one eye looking towards the land. She felt that she could see the hunters approaching her on land, and often escaped them by this means. But finally the hunters discovered that she was blind in one eye, and hiring a boat, they rowed under the cliff where she was feeding and shot her from the sea.

You cannot escape your fate.

The Man and the Serpent

A COUNTRYMAN'S SON once by accident trod upon a serpent's tail, and the serpent turned and bit him so that he died. The grieving countryman fetched his axe, and pursuing the serpent, managed to cut off part of his tail. In return the serpent dispatched several of the man's cattle, and caused him still further loss. At last the man thought it best to make his peace with the serpent, and bringing food and honey to the mouth of his lair, he said to him, "Let us forget and forgive. You were, perhaps, correct in punishing my son and taking vengeance on my cattle, but I, surely, was right in trying to revenge him. Now that we are both satisfied why should we not be friends again?"

"No, no," replied the serpent, "take away your gifts. You can never forget the death of your son, nor I the loss of my tail."

Injuries may be forgiven, but not forgotten.

The Archer and the Lion

AN ARCHER went up into the hills to sport with his bow, and all the animals fled at his sight, with the exception of the lion, who remained behind and challenged him to a fight. But the archer shot an arrow at the lion and hit him, and said, "See what my messenger can do; just you wait a moment and I'll tackle you myself."

The lion, however, when he felt the pain of the arrow, ran away as fast as his legs could carry him. A fox, who had seen the whole affair, asked the lion, "Come, don't be a coward! Why don't you stay and fight?"

But the lion replied, "You won't get me to stay, not you. Why when he sends a messenger like that before him, he must himself be a most terrible fellow to deal with."

Give a wide berth to those who can damage at a distance.

The Dog and the Hare

A HOUND dog, having startled a hare on the hillside, pursued her for some distance, sometimes nipping at her with his teeth as though he would take her life, other times fawning upon her as if in play with another dog. Finally the hare said to him, "I wish you would act sincerely and show yourself to me in your true colours. If, in fact, you are a friend, why do you bite me so hard? If you are an enemy, why do you fawn on me so?"

There are no friends whom you know not whether to trust or distrust.

The Crab and the Fox

A CRAB, forsaking the familiar neighbourhood of the sea-shore, selected an adjacent green meadow as his new feeding ground. A fox came across him, and being very much famished, commenced to eat him up. Just as he was about to be eaten, the crab cried out, "I well deserve my fate, for what business had I on the land, when by my nature and habits I am only fit for the sea?"

Contentment with our lot is an element of happiness.

The Hawk and the Nightingale

A NIGHTINGALE was once sitting high upon an oak and singing sweetly according to his custom, when he was spotted by a passing hawk in need of food. The hawk rushed down and seized him with a great swoop, but the nightingale pleaded for his life, insisting to the hawk that he was too small to satisfy his hunger, and that he should really pursue the bigger birds. The hawk, interrupting his appeal, said, "I should indeed have lost my senses if I let go food so ready to my hand, for the sake of pursuing birds which are not even yet within sight."

Men argue, nature acts.

The Flea and the Man

A FLEA bit a man, and he bit him again and again, until the man could stand it no longer, but he made a most thorough search and at last succeeded in catching him. Holding the flea in front of him between his finger and his thumb, he said—or rather he shouted, so angry was he—"Who are you, pray tell, you wretched little creature, that you dare to make so free with my person?"

The flea, terrified, whispered in a weak little voice, "Oh sir! Pray let me go. Don't kill me, for I am such a little thing that I cannot do you much harm."

But the man laughed loudly and said, "I am going to kill you now, at once. Whatever is bad must be destroyed, no matter how slight the harm it does."

Do not waste your pity on a scamp.

The Bee and Jupiter

A BEE from Mount Hymettus, the queen of the hive, ascended to Olympus, to present to Jupiter some honey fresh from her combs. Jupiter, delighted with the offering of honey, promised to give her whatever she should ask. She therefore spoke her want, saying "Give me, I pray thee, a sting, that if any mortal shall approach to take my honey, I may kill him."

Jupiter was much displeased, for he greatly loved the race of men, but could not refuse the request on account of his promise. Thus in answer to the bee he said, "You shall have your request, but you shall have it at the peril of your own life. For if you use your sting, it shall remain in the wound you make, and then you will die from the loss of it."

Evil wishes, like chickens, come home to roost.

The Pomegranate, the Apple Tree, and the Bramble

THE POMEGRANATE and the apple tree once had a dispute as to which of them was the most beautiful. When their argument was at its height, a bramble bush from the neighbouring hedge lifted up his voice, and said in a boastful tone, "Pray, my dear friends, in my presence at least to cease from such vain disputes."

Man is what he believes.

The Lion and the Three Bulls

THREE BULLS had shared a pasture together for a long time. A lion lay waiting in ambush in the hopes of making them his prey, but was afraid to pounce on them while they kept together. Having at last by treacherous speeches succeeded in separating them, he attacked each without fear as he fed alone, and feasted on them one by one, at his own leisure.

Union is strength.

The Fisherman and the Little Fish

A FISHERMAN, who lived on the produce of his nets, once day caught only a single small fish for all of his day's labour. The fish, suffering terribly in the air, entreated the fisherman for his life. "Oh sir, what good can I be to you, and how little am I worth? I am not yet come to my full size. If you spare my life, and put me back into the sea, I shall soon become a large fish, fit fare for the tables of the rich, and then you can catch me again and make a very handsome profit."

The fisherman replied, "I should indeed a very simple fellow, if,. for the chance of a greater and uncertain profit, I were to forego my present and certain gain."

No man does anything from a single motive.

The Dog and the Oyster

A DOG who was used to eating eggs saw an oyster, and, opening his mouth to its widest extent, swallowed it down with the utmost relish, supposing it to be an egg. Suffering great pains in his stomach soon afterwards, he cried, "I deserve all this torment for my folly in thinking that everything round must be an egg."

Those who act without sufficient thought will often fall into unsuspected danger.

The Viper and the File

A VIPER, entering the workshop of a blacksmith, sought from the tools there the means of satisfying his hunger. He most particularly addressed himself to a file, and asked of him the favour of a meal. The file replied, "You must indeed be a simple-minded fellow if you expect to get anything from me, who am accustomed to take from everyone, and never to give anything in return."

The covetous are poor givers.

The Shepherd and the Sheep

A SHEPHERD, driving his sheep to a wood, saw an oak of unusual size, full of acorns, and, spreading his cloak under the branches, he climbed up into the tree, and shook down them down. But the sheep inadvertently frayed and tore the cloak in their eagerness to eat the acorns. When the shepherd came down from the tree and saw what had occurred, he said, "O you most ungrateful creatures. You provide wool to make garments for all other men, but must you destroy the clothes of the one who feeds you?"

Lessons are not given, they are taken.

The Bat, the Bramble, and the Seagull

A BAT, a bramble bush, and a seagull went into partnership and determined to go a trading voyage together. The bat borrowed a sum of money for the venture; the bramble laid in a stock of clothes of various sorts; and the seagull procured a quantity of lead. So they set out, and by and by a great storm came on, and their boat, with all of its cargo, went to the bottom of the sea. The three travellers managed to reach land, but ever since then, the seagull flies to and fro over the sea, and every now and then he dives below the surface, looking for the lead he lost. The bat is now so afraid of meeting his creditors that he hides away by day and only comes out at night to feed, and the bramble bush catches hold of the clothes of every passer-by, hoping someday to recognize and recover his lost garments.

All men are more concerned to recover what they lose than to acquire what they lack.

The Gnat and the Lion

A GNAT flew up to a lion and said, "I do not the least fear you, nor are you stronger than I. For of what does your strength consist? You can scratch with your claws, and bite with your teeth—so can a woman in her quarrels. I repeat that I am altogether more powerful than you, and if you doubt me, let us fight and see who will win."

The gnat, having sounded his horn, fastened himself upon the lion, and stung him on the nostrils and the parts of his face devoid of hair. The lion, trying to crush him, tore himself severely with his claws. Thus the little gnat prevailed over the great lion, and, buzzing about in a song of triumph, flew away.

But shortly afterwards he became entangled in the threads of a cobweb, and was eaten by a spider. He greatly lamented his fate, saying, "Woe is me, that I, who can wage war successfully with the king of the beasts, should meet my end from this spider, the most insignificant of insects!"

Force is not a remedy.

The Traveller and his Dog

A TRAVELLER, about to set off on his journey, saw his dog standing idly at the door stretching himself. He asked him sharply, "What do you stand there gaping for? Everything is ready but you, now come with me instantly!" The dog, wagging his tail, replied, "O master, I am quite ready. It is you I am waiting for."

The loiterer often attributes delay to his more active friend.

The Stag and the Vine

A STAG, pursued by huntsmen, concealed himself under the covering offered by a thick vine. The men lost track of him and passed by his hiding-place without realizing he was anywhere near. Supposing all danger to have passed, the stag presently began to browse on the attractive leaves of the vine. His movement drew the attention of the returning huntsmen, and one of them, believing some animal to be hidden within, shot an arrow at a venture into the foliage. The unfortunate stag was pierced to the heart, and, as he expired, he said, "I deserve my fate for my treachery in feeding upon the leaves of my protector."

Ingratitude sometimes brings its own punishment.

The Swallow, the Serpent, and the Court of Justice

A SWALLOW, returning from abroad, and ever fond of dwelling with men, built herself a nest in the wall of a Court of Justice, and there hatched seven young birds. A serpent, passing the nest on the way to his hole in the wall, found the young hatchlings and ate them. Finding her nest empty, the swallow lamented greatly, exclaiming, "Woe to me a stranger, that in this place where all others' rights are protected, I alone should suffer a wrong."

The cold-blooded possess a poisonous bite.

The Ass and the Frogs

AN ASS, carrying a load of wood, was compelled to pass through a pond. As he was crossing through the water he lost his footing, and stumbled and fell, and being unable to rise on account of his heavy load, he began to groan loudly. The frogs, who frequent that pond, heard his lamentations, and remarked, "What would you do if you had to live here always as we do, when you make such a fuss about a mere fall into the water?"

Men often bear little grievances with less courage than they do large misfortunes.

The Birdcatcher, the Partridge, and the Cock

A BIRDCATCHER was just about to sit down to a meager dinner of herbs, when a friend came unexpectedly to visit. The bird-trap was quite empty, as he had caught nothing, so he prepared to kill a pied partridge, which he had tamed for a decoy. The partridge pleaded earnestly for his life, saying, "What would you do without me when next you spread your nets? Who would chirp you so sweetly to sleep, or call for you the covey of answering birds?"

The birdcatcher therefore decided to spare his life, and went to pick out a fine young cock just attaining to his comb. But the cock cried in piteous tones from his perch, "If you kill me, who will announce to you the appearance of the dawn? Who will wake you to your daily tasks, or tell you when it is time to visit the bird-trap in the mornings?"

The birdcatcher replied, "What you say is true. You are a most useful bird for telling the time of day. But I and my friend who has come to visit must have our dinner."

Necessity knows no law.

The Mouse and the Bull

A BULL once gave chase to a mouse who had bitten him on the nose, but the mouse was far too quick for him, and slipped into a hole in the wall. The bull charged furiously into the wall again and again until he was spent, and sank down on the ground exhausted with his efforts. When all was quiet, the mouse darted out and bit him again. Beside himself with rage, the bull started to his feet, but by that time the mouse had returned to his hole again, and there was nothing he could do but bellow and fume in helpless anger. Presently he heard a shrill little voice speak up from inside the wall, "You big fellows don't always have it your way, sometimes we little ones come off best."

The battle is not always won by the strong.

The Master and his Dogs

A MAN, compelled to keep to his country house by the ravages of a fierce winter storm, first killed his sheep, and then all of his goats, for the maintenance of his household. The storm continued to rage, and he was obliged to slaughter even his yoke oxen for food. On seeing this, his dogs took counsel together, and said, "It is time for us to be off, for if our master spares not his oxen, who work for his gain, how can we expect him to spare us?"

He is not to be trusted as a friend who mistreats his own family.

The Farmer and the Snake

A FARMER found in the winter time a snake stiff and frozen with cold. He took pity on him, and picking him up, placed him in his bosom. Thawed by the warmth, the snake quickly revived, and resuming his natural instincts, he sharply bit his benefactor, inflicting on him a mortal wound. The farmer said with his dying breath, "I am rightly served for pitying a scoundrel."

The greatest benefits will not bind the ungrateful.

The Stag and the Lion

A STAG was chased by hounds, and found refuge in a nearby cave, where he hoped to be safe from his pursuers. Unfortunately the cave contained a lion, to whom he fell an easy prey. "Unhappy that I am," he cried, "I am saved from the dogs only to fall into the clutches of a lion."

Out of the frying pan into the fire.

The Fox and the Mosquitoes

A FOX was crossing a river when his tail became entangled in a bush, and he could not move any farther. Seeing his plight, a vast number of mosquitoes settled upon him to enjoy a good meal undisturbed by the motion of his tail. A hedgehog strolling by took pity upon the fox, and coming up to him, said, "Neighbour, you seem to be in a bad way! Shall I assist you by driving off these mosquitoes who are sucking your blood?"

"Thank you, master hedgehog," said Reynard, "but I would rather not."

"Why, how is that?" asked the hedgehog.

"Well, you see," was the reply, "these mosquitoes have had their fill; if you drive them away, others will come with fresh appetite and bleed me to death."

War can protect, it cannot create.

The Two Frogs

THERE once were two frogs who dwelt together in the same pool. The pool being dried up under the heat of

ÆSOP'S FABLES

the summer sun, they left it, and set forth to find another home. As they walked along they chanced to pass a deep well, amply supplied with water, on seeing which one of the frogs said to the other, "Let us descend and make our abode in this well; it will furnish us with shelter and food." The other frog replied with greater caution, "But suppose the water should fail us, how can we get out again from so great a depth?"

Do nothing without regard to the consequences.

The Lion, the Mouse, and the Fox

A LION, fatigued by the heat of a summer's day, fell fast asleep in his den until a mouse ran right over his mane and ears, and rudely woke him from his slumbers. He rose up and shook himself in great wrath, and searched in every corner of his den to find the mouse. A fox, seeing him in this state, said, "A fine lion you are, to be frightened of a mouse."

"'Tis not the mouse I fear," replied the lion, "I resent his familiarity and ill-breeding."

Little liberties are great offenses.

The She-Goats and their Beards

THE SHE-GOATS having obtained by petition from Jupiter the favour of a beard, the he-goats complained in displeasure that the she-goats would now equal them in dignity. "Suffer them," replied Jupiter, "to enjoy this empty honour, and to assume the badge of your nobler sex, so long as they are not your equals in strength or courage."

It matters little if those who are inferior to us in merit should be like us in outside appearances.

The Wolves and the Dogs

ONCE upon a time the wolves said to the dogs, "Why should we continue to be enemies any longer? You are very like us in most ways; the real difference between us is one of training only. We live a life of freedom, but you are enslaved to mankind, who beat you, and put heavy collars around your necks. Men compel you to keep watch over their flocks and herds for them, and to make matters worse, they give you nothing but bones to eat. Do not put up with it any longer, but hand over the flocks to us, and we will all live on the fat of the land and feast together."

The dogs allowed themselves to be persuaded by these words, and accompanied the wolves into their den. But no sooner were they well inside then the wolves set upon them and tore them to pieces.

Traitors richly deserve their fate.

The Widow and the Sheep

A CERTAIN poor widow possessed only one sheep. At sheering time, wishing to take his fleece, but to avoid expense, she sheared him herself, but used the sheers with so little skill that along with the fleece she sheared his flesh. The sheep, writhing with pain, said, "Why do you hurt me so, O mistress? What weight can my blood add to the wool? If you want my flesh, there is the butcher, who will kill me in a trice, but if you want my fleece and wool, there is the shearer, who will shear and not hurt me."

The least outlay is not always the greatest gain.

The Blind Man and the Cub

THERE once was a blind man who had so fine a sense of touch that, whenever any animal was put into his hands, he could name it merely by the feel of it. One day the cub of a wolf was put into his hands, and he was asked to say what sort of animal it was. He felt it for some time, and then said, "Indeed, I am not sure whether it is a wolf's cub or the cub of a fox, but this I know—it would never do to trust it in a sheepfold."

Evil tendencies are shown early.

The Blacksmith and his Dog

A BLACKSMITH had a little dog, which was a great favourite with his master, and his constant companion. While he hammered away at his work the dog slept, but when, on the other hand, he went to dinner and began to eat, the dog promptly awoke, and wagging his tail, would ask for a share of the meal. His master one day, pretending to be angry, and shaking his stick at him, said, "You wretched little sluggard! What shall I do to you? While I am hammering on the anvil, you sleep on the mat; and when I begin to eat after my toils, you wake up, and wag your tail for food. Do you not know that labour is the source of every blessing, and that none but those who work are entitled to eat?"

He who can lick, can bite.

The Swallow and the Other Birds

IT happened that a farmer was sowing hemp seeds in the same field where a swallow and some birds were hopping about to pick up their food. "Beware of that man," advised the swallow to the other birds.

"Why, what is he doing?" they replied.

"The seed he is sowing is hemp; be careful to pick up every last one of the seeds, or you will live to regret it."

The birds paid no attention to the swallow's warning, and by and by the hemp sprouted, and grew up, and was made into cords, and of the cords nets were fashioned, and many a bird that had despised the swallow's advice was caught in nets made from that very hemp.

"What did I tell you?" said the swallow.

Destroy the seed of evil, or it will grow up to your ruin.

The Ass and his Burdens

A PEDDLER who owned an ass one day bought up a quantity of salt, and loaded his beast with as much as he could bear. Crossing a stream on the way home, the ass stumbled, and fell into the water. The salt was thoroughly wetted and much of it melted right away, so that, when the ass managed to get on his legs again, he found his load had become much less burdensome. His master, however, drove him back to town and bought more salt, to which he added what remained in his baggage, and they started out again. No sooner had they reached the stream than the ass lay down in it, and rose, as before, with a much lightened load. His master finally detected the trick, and turning back once more, purchased a large quantity of sponges, and piled them on the back of the ass. When they came to the stream for the third time, the ass lay down, but, as the sponges soaked up large quantities of water, he found that when he got to his legs, that he had a bigger burden to carry than ever.

You can play a good card once too often.

The Farmer and the Stork

A FARMER placed nets on his newly sown fields, and caught a quantity of cranes, who had come to pick up the seeds. With them he also trapped a stork. The stork, having his leg fractured by the net, entreated the farmer to spare his life. "Pray save me, master," he said, "and let me go free this once. My broken leg should touch your sympathy. Besides, I am no crane, I am a stork, a bird of most excellent character; see how I love and slave for my mother and father. Look, too, at my feathers, for they are not the least like those of a crane."

The farmer laughed aloud, and said, "It may be all as you say, but I only know this, that I have taken you with these robbers, the cranes, and you must die in their company."

Birds of a feather flock together.

The Hawk, the Kite, and the Pigeons

THE PIGEONS, terrified by the appearance of a fearsome kite, called upon a hawk to defend them. He at once consented, but when they had admitted him into their cote, they found that he made more havoc and slew a larger number of them in one day alone, than the kite could have dispatched in an entire year.

Avoid a remedy that is worse than the disease.

The Rivers and the Sea

THE RIVERS decided one day to join together and complain to the sea, saying, "Why is it that when our waters flow so sweetly into your tides that you change us to salty brine and so render us unfit to drink?"

The sea, perceiving that they intended to blame him for the matter, replied, "Pray cease to flow into me, and then you will not become brine."

Some will always find fault with the things that benefit them.

The Lion and the Fox

A FOX entered in a partnership with a lion, on the pretence of becoming his servant. Each undertook his proper duty in accordance with his own nature and powers. The fox discovered and pointed out the prey; the lion sprung upon it, and seized it. But Reynard soon became jealous of the lion carrying off the largest portion of the spoil, and said that he would no longer hunt out the prey for him, but would capture it solely on his own account. The very next day he attempted to snatch a lamb from the fold, but himself fell prey to the huntsmen and the hounds.

Even the wise must recognize their limits.

The Stag in the Ox-Stall

A STAG, hotly pursued by the hounds, took refuge in an ox-stall, and buried himself in a bale of hay, leaving nothing to be seen but the tips of his horns. Soon afterwards the hunters came up and asked if any one had seen the stag. The stable boys, who had been resting after their dinner, looked around, but could see nothing, and the hunters went away with empty hands. Shortly thereafter, the farmer walked in, and looking around, saw that something out of the ordinary had occurred. He pointed to the bale of hay and said, "What is that there sticking up out of the hay?"

When the stable boys came up to look, they promptly discovered the stag, and so made an end of him.

Nothing escapes the master's eye.

The Rose and the Amaranth

AN AMARANTH was planted in a garden next to a rose tree, and he addressed his neighbour, saying, "What a lovely flower is the rose, a favourite alike with gods and with men. How I envy you your beauty and your perfume."

The dainty rose replied, "I, indeed, dear amaranth, flourish but for a brief season! If no cruel hand should pluck me from my stem, yet I must perish by an early doom. But thou, thou art immortal, and do never fade, but bloom forever in renewed youth."

The flower in the vase smiles, but it can no longer laugh.

The Trees under the Protection of the Gods

THE GODS, according to ancient legend, made a choice of certain trees to be under their divine protection. Jupiter chose the oak, Venus the myrtle, Apollo the laurel, Cybele the pine, and Hercules the poplar. Minerva, wondering why they had preferred trees not yielding fruit, inquired the reason for their choice. Jupiter replied, "It is lest we should seem to covet the honour for the fruit."

"But," said Minerva, "the olive is much more dear to me on account of its fruit."

"Then," said Jupiter, "my daughter, you are rightly called wise, for unless what we do is useful, the glory of it is in vain."

To know the world one must construct it.

The Mice and the Weasels

THE MICE and the weasels waged perpetual warfare with each other, in which much blood was shed. The weasels were always the victors, and the mice believed that the cause of their frequent defeats was that they had not appointed leaders set apart from the general army to command them, and that they were further exposed to dangers from great want of discipline. They chose, therefore, such mice as were most renowned for their family descent, strength, and council, as well as those most noted for their courage in battle, so that they might marshal the rest in fighting array, and form them into troops, regiments, and battalions. When all of this had been done, and the army was disciplined, the herald mouse duly proclaimed war by challenging the weasels. The newly chosen generals bound their heads with straws that they might be conspicuous to all their troops. Scarcely had the battle commenced, when a great rout overwhelmed the mice, who scampered off as fast as they could go to their holes. The generals, being unable to enter because of the straws on their heads, were all captured and eaten by the weasels.

The more honour the more danger.

The Goat and the Goatherd

A GOATHERD sought to bring back a stray goat to his flock. He whistled and blew his horn in vain, for the straggler paid no attention to his summons. At last the goatherd threw a stone at him, and breaking the goat's horn, pleaded with him not to tell his master. The goat replied, "Why, you silly man, the horn will speak even if I am silent."

Do not attempt to hide things which cannot be hidden.

The Mouse, the Frog, and the Hawk

A MOUSE, who had always lived on the land, by an unlucky chance formed an intimate acquaintance with a frog, who lived for the most part in the water. Intent on mischief one day, the frog bound the mouse's foot tightly to his own, and thus joined together, he first led his friend the mouse to the meadow where they were accustomed to find their food. After this, he took him towards the pool where he lived, until he reached the very edge, and suddenly jumped in, dragging the mouse along with him. The frog enjoyed the water amazingly, and swam croaking about, as if he had done a meritorious deed. The unhappy mouse was soon drowned in the water, and floated about on the surface of the pond still attached to the leg of the frog. A passing hawk spotted the prize, and pouncing upon it with his talons, he carried the dead mouse off into the sky. The miserable frog, still fastened to his leg, was also taken prisoner, and made a meal of by the hawk.

Harm hatch, harm catch.

The Lion and the Statue

A MAN and a lion were discussing the relative strength of men and lions in general. The man contended that he and his fellow men were stronger than lions by reason of their greater intelligence. When the lion objected, and demanded proof of the premise, the man declared, "Come with me now, and I will soon show you that I am right." And he took him right then and there into the public gardens and showed him a statue of Hercules overcoming the lion and tearing his mouth in two.

"That is all very well," said the lion, "but proves nothing, for it was, after all, a man who made the statue."

We can easily represent things
as we wish them to be.

The Monkey as King

AT a gathering of all the animals the monkey danced and delighted them so much that they made him their king. The fox, however, was very much disgusted at the promotion of the monkey, so having one day found a trap with a piece of meat in it, he took the monkey to the spot and said to him, "Here is a dainty morsel I have found, sire. I did not take it myself, because I thought it ought to be reserved for you, our king. Will you be so pleased as to accept it?"

The monkey made at once for the meat and got caught in the trap. Then he bitterly reproached the fox for leading him into danger, but Reynard only laughed and said, "O monkey, you call yourself king of the beasts and haven't more sense than to be taken in like that!"

The secure are most likely to be hurt.

The Cat-Maiden

THE GODS were once disputing whether it was possible for a living being to change its nature. Jupiter said "Yes," but Venus said "No," and to test the question, Jupiter decided to transform a cat into a maiden, and he gave her to a young man as his wife. The wedding ceremonies were duly performed, and the young couple had at last sat down to their wedding feast. "See," said Jupiter to Venus, "how beautifully she behaves. Who could tell that only yesterday she was but a cat? Surely her nature has changed?"

"Pray wait a minute," replied Venus, and she let loose a mouse into the room. No sooner did the bride spot the mouse than she jumped up from her seat and pounced upon the mouse.

Nature will triumph over all.

The Lamp

A LAMP, soaked with too much oil, and flaring very much, boasted that he gave more light than even the sun. A sudden puff of wind arising, he was immediately extinguished. His owner lit him again, and said, "Boast no more, but henceforth be content to give your light in silence. Know that not even the stars need to be relit."

Vanity is the greatest of all flatterers.